R. Oily

Eanymore

L. F...

Bannesmore

Milltown

Mountcharles

R. Eask

R.

Inver B.
Doorin Pt.

a l Bay

Ballintra

Layd...

Pettigoe

Tu...

Ballyshannon

R.

Belleek

Bunderan

R. Drowes

Erne

L. Erne

1149

L. Melvin

Church Hill

Kinlough

R. Duff

Garrison

Derrygonnelly

Mon...

...iffony

20

R. Roogah

L. Ross

...nge

L. Glenade

1408

L

846

Glencar L.

Kiltyclogher

1511

Ulpr

E

F

1312

...mcliff

1524

Manor
Hamilton

Lurganboy

L. Macnean

...tron

Sligo

14.50

L.

L. Gill

Black Lion

Nilly

Gill

Drumahaire

1417

E

170

20

L. Belhavel

1448

Shannon

Cuilcagh

2188

...ally sadare

Drumkeeran

R.

Slievena

Killa

1793

O

Ballintogher

Br...

1498

L. Allen

1707

Benbr...

1648

...binbe

Riverstown

1163

Bencroy

Ba...

...berscanavan

Arigna

1952

L.

Ballymag

...allymote

1098

Am...

Ballinam...

Drumshanbo

L.

Arrow

Keadew

R.

Shannon

...altinafad

Leitrim

Fenagh

Carlew

L.

M...

Shan...

...Boyle

Cootehall

Erne

&

Cap...

Foster and Allen
Singing Duo

We are thrilled to be given the honour of writing this segment for our good friend Henry's book. It is clear from reading his intriguing life story that he has lived and enjoyed a truly amazing life and that Henry has always had a passion for the radio both as a listener and broadcaster.

He has pioneered the voice of the Irish in the UK over the last twenty years, and played an important role in promoting Irish culture and music to the millions. Any visit to see Henry in the BBC studio is a special treat, with his warmth and relaxing personality. I suppose the best way to describe the whole experience is of a casual living room chat – easy going, just like the great man himself.

A must read for everyone!

Mick and Tony

Graham Clifford
Feature Writer, Irish Independent Newspaper

Few life journeys have taken as many unexpected twists and turns as that of Henry Wymbs – a reality so perfectly illustrated in this outstanding autobiography. Indeed there are so many great sides to Henry that he's a people magnet in front of and away from the microphone. A man who combines sincerity and roguishness in equal measure to always evoke a smile. His story mirrors the transition that took place for Irish people in England over a generation. Henry took me under his wing at the BBC and for six years helped me along when I'd present *Irish Eye* in his stead. We were forever talking GAA, with Henry telling me of the greats who lit up his world as a boy in his beloved *áit dúchais* (native place) of Sligo. A gentleman, gifted writer and broadcaster and never one to shy away from a challenge, this piece of work is yet another splendid success to which his name is attached.

Graham

Daniel O'Donnell
Singer and Entertainer

It is with great pleasure that I write these few words to be included in Henry's book. I first met Henry when he interviewed me for his radio programme *Irish Eye*. We hit it off immediately and we have had many enjoyable meetings in the intervening years. As you will see from reading his memoirs he has had quite a journey, from his early years in Ireland to his life as a policeman and then on to his time entertaining people over the airwaves on the BBC.

I'm so glad he decided to write this book. It gives us an insight into the life of a man who has the ability to connect with people in a very special way.

Henry, it has been a pleasure getting to know you. I look forward to many more meetings in the future.

Daniel

A Wymbsical Journey

To Keith & Steve

"Best Wishes"

I would like to thank my wife, Sally and two sons, Duncan and Stephen, whose frank and helpful thoughts and comments contributed greatly in shaping this book.

A Wymbsical Journey

... the Eventful Life Story of BBC Radio Presenter
Henry Wymbs

by
Henry Wymbs

AN OXFORDFOLIO PUBLICATION

An Oxfordfolio publication
(www.oxfordfolio.co.uk)

Design/typesetting: Forewords, www.forewords.co.uk
Jacket design: Nick Allen
Colophons: Hugo Harrison
Project editor: James Harrison
All images © the author
Press cuttings by kind permission of Newsquest Media Group
Limited (and Regional Editor, Gary Lawrence)
Extract from "My Father's House" (1986) by Kevin Sherrin,
reproduced with kind permission
Extract from "I've Always Been Crazy" (1978) by Waylon Jennings,
Sony Music/RCA Records

10 9 8 7 6 5 4 3 2 1

A CIP catalogue record for this book is available from the
British Library
ISBN: 9780956740595

Typeset in 11/16.5 point Adobe Caslon Pro

Printed and bound in the United Kingdom by TJ International, Padstow
on TJ Woodfree Cream paper

Front flap illustration courtesy of Chris Payne

Henry Wymbs is also the author of *Eire Og – 50 Years of Gaelic
Games in Oxford* (still available)

Contents

Prologue

As I looked up I could see two people walking towards me in the distance. On coming into view, I was surprised to see that one of them was my mother, Nancy. It was 1964 and I was working part-time in a hotel near my hometown of Sligo on the west coast of Ireland; I wasn't expecting visitors. Nancy was in the company of a well-heeled man, whom I immediately recognised from the newspaper as one of Ireland's national basketball coaches. I had never played the game before – funnily enough basketball doesn't suit those that are vertically challenged – but I remained optimistic: perhaps he had heard of my exploits on the football field and wanted me to try out his sport?

He hadn't! I soon learnt that the basketball coach was, in fact, there in a completely different capacity, as the sales manager of Maye's Motors in Sligo. Nancy then turned to me and proudly announced that she had purchased a new Hillman Imp motor car from the man. I was shocked and bemused. Who exactly was the car for? Nancy couldn't ride a bike properly, let alone drive, and my father Michael could only drive a cub tractor – nothing more than a dinky toy for adults. My excitement at the prospect of the car potentially being for me quickly evaporated when I was informed that, in Nancy's wheeling and dealing, she had thrown me in as part of the deal. I was to take on an apprenticeship as a panel beater in the man's garage. No interviews, start in a month's time. I was now more bemused than ever. What did a panel beater do? The man sat me down and explained that the job involved repairing and spraying damaged cars and that full training would be provided.

On leaving the hotel that evening and looking out towards the rolling countryside and Atlantic Ocean beyond, I reflected on my life thus far. With a four-year apprenticeship on offer and a serious lack of other opportunities – with limited education and experience heads of large companies were hardly knocking on my door – I had no choice but to grin and bear it. Aged seventeen, I would take the job, but in my heart I knew that this was not my future...

Introduction

Over the years I have often sat down with my two sons, Duncan and Stephen, and reminisced about my past. My childhood days growing up in rural Ireland as the eldest of ten children; moving to England in the late sixties to work for the police; and, in more recent years, working on the radio as presenter of the BBC's *Irish Eye* programme. I now enjoy telling these same tales to my grandchildren. My darling wife, Sally, has heard the stories so many times she could probably recount the numerous tales in her own book. Anyway, now getting on in years, and age not quenching the spark within, I decided, with the arrival of my latest little grandson, Ralph, to delve into the memory bank and put pen to paper.

I started scribbling down a few thoughts and, as the days went by and the ideas kept coming thick and fast, I was amazed by how much I could remember. In fact, the writing process soon became all consuming – I would find myself waking up in the early hours of the morning remembering a tale worthy of inclusion in this book. Downstairs I would rush to my computer to transfer the ideas from head to screen before the tiredness kicked in and the story returned to the back of a willing, but ageing brain. This routine went on for a number of months until I had finally finished the first draft. At this point the amount I had written was far beyond what I had ever expected. Of course whether the words are any good is really up to you, the reader, to decide!

My story begins by covering life growing up in Ireland from the late 1940s through to the 1960s. This nostalgic look back will remind those brought up then of a unique time that once was theirs; and, for others, it will introduce them to a village life they probably never thought existed. I then move on to cover my life in England, starting with me joining the Oxford city police force in the late 1960s and experiencing the ups and downs of a thirty-year career on the beat and as a detective. From there I talk about my years from the mid-1990s to the present day working in the media, including my time as a police press officer, columnist for the *Irish Post* newspaper and eventually producer and presenter on BBC radio. Finally, my life story turns full circle and sees me focusing on present day Ireland, reflecting on how life has changed in my hometown, and talking a little about my immediate family.

Whilst I have sought to be as open and transparent as possible, given the sensitivities associated with police work, I have deliberately not disclosed the names of individual police officers to preserve their anonymity. Most of the material in this book is not in the public domain. It's gleaned from my own personal experience of life in Ireland and England, from conversations with my family, and the accumulation of nearly seventy years of living a wonderful life.

Photographs provide a particularly poignant reminder of the 'good old days', and for this book I have managed, with the help of family and friends, to compile some snapshots of people and places which I hope help to bring some of the stories to life.

Looking back now, to a young, eager but naive boy growing up in Ireland, I could never have imagined all the places my life would take me and all the incredible people I would meet through my work in the police and BBC. Many, including heroes of my childhood, such as Irish showband stars and my beloved hurlers and footballers (Gaelic, not soccer), I now call friends.

In many ways, my life story reflects the experiences of the tens of thousands of people that left rural Ireland in the 1950s and 1960s in search of work. Moreover, it deals with the common threads that unite all people who have travelled away from their birthplace to a new country, exploring themes such as hope, and the desire to forge out a better future; companionship, and building new relationships whilst striving to retain those that have been left behind; and remembrance, in terms of embracing future change but not losing sight of the past.

With this in mind, I hope that my life story will provide an interesting – and entertaining – insight into what it has been like adjusting from Irish farm life to the hustle and bustle of police and radio work. I also hope it keeps my family heritage alive so that the stories contained within can be read and enjoyed by future generations.

Chapter One

MY IRISH ROOTS

MY BEGINNINGS

The year of my birth, 1947, saw one of the biggest snowfalls ever recorded in my hometown of Sligo on the west coast of Ireland. In fact, the year still holds the record as being the coldest in living memory. Only those folk now in their late seventies or older will remember it. The blizzard, which began stealthily in the form of heavy snow showers in early spring, is unlikely to be forgotten by any surviving soul who suffered its merciless fury. My father, Michael, told me that the snow blocked the door of the house almost to the top. The snow deluge lasted for months and, unable to get out, they almost starved.

Although World War Two was over, Ireland was isolated by neutrality and still in the dark ages twenty-five years after gaining independence from Britain. The late 1940s was a difficult time for the country, with economic struggles and the start of a long period of high emigration. During the war approximately 150,000 people emigrated from Ireland in search of work and new beginnings. This figure would continue to rise and during the 1950s an estimated 400,000 Irish citizens (fifteen per cent of the population) would move away from Ireland's shores[1].

---

[1] Glynn, Irial with Tomás Kelly and Piaras Mac Éinrí, *The Re-emergence of Emigration from Ireland: New Trends in an Old Story* (Washington, DC: Migration Policy Institute 2015) <available online>.

From a historical context, 1947 was the year that Princess Elizabeth and Prince Philip got married in London, the National Health Service was established in the UK, Harry Truman was president of America and, more importantly to me in later years, Kilkenny won the All-Ireland hurling final and Cavan the All-Ireland football.

I was born on Tuesday 11th November in the townland[2] of Cloonkeen, a couple of miles from the village of Cliffoney. This small village is perched on the furthermost coast of Europe, in as remote a place as possible. It is situated about fourteen miles north of the town of Sligo and eight miles west of Bundoran, one of Ireland's top seaside resorts. The border with Northern Ireland lies east within twenty miles.

Michael married my mother, Nancy Keogh, in the mid-1940s and I was the first of their ten offspring. Like all children then, I was born at home and got to know Nurse Bennett, who delivered me, very well in later years. Believe it or not, she always said I was a cute little boy with a good head of fair hair.

According to my godmother, Granny Kate, I was quite poorly during the early weeks of my life. Mind you I shouldn't be here at all according to today's regulators and bureaucrats. Those of us who were kids back then survived despite our baby cots being covered with brightly coloured, lead-based paint which we promptly chewed and licked. In addition, I clearly remember youngsters drinking Cow & Gate milk from Guinness bottles with homemade teats. We had no childproof lids on medicine bottles, or latches on doors or cabinets, and it was fine to play with pots and pans. When we rode our bikes, we wore no helmets, with just bare feet. I'm told my daytime cradle was a tea chest, a large wooden box with silver foil on the inside which came from India full of loose tea originally destined for the local shops. The shopkeeper would have weighed the tea into brown paper bags prior to selling it on. Once empty there was a great demand for the boxes, which could be used for storage and playpens.

---

[2] In Ireland, a division of land, varying in extent according to locality; a territorial division.

As young children we had the freedom to play in the streets unafraid, where doors were left open and unlocked, and parents did not have to worry unduly. Indeed mothers would actively encourage their children to play outside to get some peace and quiet. Despite the large, precarious bog holes near the woods, we felt safe, and I recall roaming the fields and woods from an early age, sometimes not arriving back until dark. Children were never overweight when I was young and I'm sure this was because we were always outside playing. I fondly remember climbing tall trees, falling out of them, getting cut and bruised, and not a word to my mother, Nancy, about it. Nobody bothered the doctors with minor ailments. Where necessary, Nancy would simply lance a boil, and then strap a red-hot poultice over it to prevent infection. In addition, I recall being given plenty of milk of magnesia, which kept the bowels moving.

Looking back now, I realise that during my childhood there was a lot of prejudice in Irish society, which nobody was allowed to question. We had a narrow attitude towards anything that threatened our perceived feelings or security. There were stigmas attached to many things, including mental illness, children born out of wedlock and cancer. Like all prejudices, I picked them up from the environment I lived in. The words 'psychiatric hospital' were never used, but everyone knew what people were referring to when the 'mad house' or the 'lunatic asylum' were mentioned, and they put the fear of God into you.

Life was so different in 1947. I was born before the mainstream use of televisions, frozen foods, plastic, dishwashers, electric blankets, and well before man walked on the moon. Couples married first, and then lived together. A big mac was an oversized raincoat and crumpet was something we had for tea. Sheltered accommodation meant waiting for the bus and we had never heard of disposable nappies or yogurt. Only ladies wore earrings, a stud was something that fastened a collar to a shirt and, before 1947, 'made in China' meant junk. In my day cigarette smoking tended to be trendy, 'grass' was mown, and a 'joint' was something you cooked.

Those born before 1947 must have been a hardy bunch when you think of the ways in which the world has since changed and the way we have had to adjust. No wonder I get confused. By the grace of God, I'm still here to tell the tale!

THE WYMBS'

My birthplace, now a tumbledown ruin in the hamlet of Cloonkeen, and only a few fields away from where I was reared, had been a temporary home when my parents got married. We only lived there for a matter of months and then moved in with my paternal grandfather, Henry, and his brother Peter, who lived in a farmhouse along the road.

I have very little recollection of my grandfather or what he looked like – no cameras in our house of course – however, I do remember one incident with him at about the age of four, which is one of my earliest memories. Henry, whom I was named after and who was also my godfather, was by all accounts a good tradesman. Whilst he was repairing a stone wall, he asked me to hold a hammer and, like all innocent and curious children do, I started to hammer at everything

My birthplace in Cloonkeen

in sight. Unfortunately, poor old grandfather must have been in the wrong place at the wrong time as I proceeded to hit him right on the nose, causing blood to spill out everywhere. Half in fear and not knowing what to do, I ran off. Henry Senior sadly passed away the following year; however, much to my relief, the hammer blow had nothing to do with his death.

I have some hazy memories of my great uncle Peter. He was a smallish man who never got married – perhaps the reason why he always had a smile on his roguish little face. I recall that he held the purse strings as grandfather liked a little drink now and then.

My grandfather Henry had at least one sister, Ann Jane, who I clearly remember and, apart from Peter, he had one other brother called Dan who, to the best of my knowledge, lived in England. I never met him, but he had a son called Michael who would come home occasionally. Dan was a very popular name in the Wymbs family. So much so, many beyond my immediate family had nicknames like 'Red Dan', 'Black Dan', 'Big Dan' and 'Wee Dan'. It's difficult even now with access to census records online to fully resource exactly who was who. Regretfully I didn't ask enough questions when I was young to ascertain what relation they were to us. To add to their number, I now have a grandson called Dan(ny).

The surname Wymbs is quite unusual and, from what I have read, the origins can be traced back hundreds of years. The spelling is a variation on Weymes, quite popular in Sligo during the late nineteenth century. There are an abundance of different spellings of the name, including Wymes, Wimbs and Wims. Given the recent arrival of my grandson, Ralph, I was very interested to read that the earliest recorded written reference to Weymes is a Ralphy Wymes from Co. Meath, who went to the baronial court in 1306 (over seven hundred years before baby Ralph, my grandson, arrived in this world!). There are other references to the name Wymbs, particularly in the U.S. and Scotland, where the name historically originated as Wemyss[3].

---

[3]   According to the website Wemys of Ireland.

My father with my brother, Michael

My great uncle Peter died in 1956. It was the first time I saw a dead body, and I remember mother telling me to run over the road to tell a namesake of ours, Jim Wymbs, of the death. When I say 'over the road' it was actually the best part of a mile. I remember Peter's wake and funeral; I cried for weeks afterwards.

My father, Michael, inherited the house and farm of about thirty-five acres after Peter's death. Ireland at this time was dirt poor and, without the right connections, you didn't get a decent job. Consequently, my father had no access to any meaningful employment away from the farm.

Michael was the second oldest boy in a family of six children, three boys and three girls. I never knew Grandmother Wymbs, as she died very young, but a rare picture reveals a striking, beautiful lady. My three aunts all died in their twenties from the deadly tuberculosis disease which was affecting Ireland at the time. TB was an awful disease and if a family member was struck down the whole family was stigmatised.

My father's older brother – yet another Dan – emigrated to England in the 1950s. I got to know him and his lovely wife Margaret very

My father's older brother, Dan

well in later years. They lived in Macclesfield and had four children, Brendan, Mary, Anne and John.

Michael's younger brother, my Uncle Pat, lived in Cliffoney village and worked for Sligo council for many years. He was gifted with his hands and could do or make anything. Bicycle repairs was one of

My paternal grandmother, Mary Gilmartin (right), with her sister, Rosie

his many interests, although he was often persuaded to take on other tasks. Many an evening I spent in Uncle Pat's house and workshop watching him mending bikes, drinking tea and eating Wagon Wheels. Michael and Uncle Pat were very similar in build, looks and nature – smallish men, very quiet, with cursing and swearing frowned upon. I recall that short hair was the order of the day for maturing youngsters back in those days and woe betide any chap caught with a mop of unsightly hair in the presence of Uncle Pat. He would take out a pair of hair clippers and mow the mop off you.

Father's younger brother, Pat

Uncle Pat's carpentry skills were passed down to his son P.J., who is a man of many talents. Now retired, P.J. still loves to work with timber, wood turning being his speciality, using an arsenal of specialist tools (both modern and the old style lathes) to create all sorts of different shapes and ornaments. Uncle Pat was married to Madge and together they had six children: Mary, P.J., Bridie, Marion, Gerard and another Dan, who still lives in the old homestead.

Most of the Wymbs' are buried in the local Ahamlish cemetery, which is all but a shrine to me when I'm in the village.

And what about my siblings? Well, between 1947 and 1969, Nancy and Michael had ten children. It seems a large number nowadays, but back then it wasn't too uncommon. I was the eldest, followed two years later by Mary, who would be the brunt of so many of my pranks. Then there followed Pete, Pat and Thomas, all two years apart. Joan came next to break the trend and I'm sure much to the relief of Mary, and then during the 1960s came John, Martina (Tina), Michael and finally, just before the decade came to a close, the baby of the family, Ann.

Twenty-one years is a long time and a generation. By the time I was packing my bags for England in January 1968, Tina was a three-year-old toddler, Michael was six months old and my sister Ann was not even on the scene. For that reason many of my earlier childhood memories really only feature Mary or my three oldest brothers, all of whom were born in the 1950s.

THE KEOGHs

My mother Nancy (christened Ann) was a huge character and I suppose some of my craziness comes from her. She came from a family of two boys and five girls.

Nancy's mother, my grandmother Kathleen Haran, married a man by the name of Peter Keogh who died young and is believed to be buried in Manchester. Granny Kate, as I always called her, was a remarkable woman who worked as a housekeeper for a dentist in Cookstown, Co. Tyrone for many years. She frequently visited our house. It was well known amongst the extended family that I was one of her favourite grandchildren. Bless her, she always gave me money, especially when I became a teenager. My brother Pat would be curious when Granny Kate would shake my hand, knowing that a ten bob note had been passed to me. She always had a fag in her mouth and, bearing in mind this was well before the introduction of filter cigarettes, her fingers were stained a dark brown. Granny Kate

My mother, Nancy (right), with her sister, Rosie, and brother Peter in
Cloonkeen in the early 1960s

came to live with my parents in the late 1960s and died there in
1991 at the ripe old age of ninety.

My uncle Kevin Keogh was the oldest of my mother's siblings
and one of the great characters around the village and surrounding
areas. He was a marvellous storyteller and at times would appear to
make them up as he went along. Some of the tales are legendary, like
'hurricane Debbie', the most powerful storm ever to hit Ireland in

My maternal grandfather, Peter

September 1961. I remember the storm well myself and hid under the table in our kitchen for hours. Kevin, in his own words, was looking out of his kitchen window onto a field of freshly mown hay. He could see the farmer on top of what we called a 'tram-cock' of hay about four metres high and tied down with ropes. The next thing the hay and the man were blown up towards the sky, and were found hours later in Killybegs, a fishing port some forty miles away. According to Kevin the farmer was still on top of the hay!

Looking back, there were literally hundreds of funny yarns like this, enough to fill a book. Although you wouldn't always be sure which ones were true – difficult to tell fact from fiction with Kevin – one thing was for sure, you would always be entertained. Kevin liked to socialise and his storytelling was like a magnet that attracted people to him. In fact, I rarely saw him on his own. Whenever I could I would drop in to see him in Cliffoney and, even though I had heard the same yarns hundreds of times, he could still make me laugh. Many's the time my intended five minute visit would be extended by a couple of hours and several glasses of Jameson whiskey as I listened to more extraordinary tales.

For a while Kevin lived by the side of a local tourist attraction,

Kevin and Sally in O'Donnells Pub

Creevykeel Court Tomb, one of the best examples of a court cairn in Ireland, and I have happy memories of spending time in the evenings with him climbing the great boulders and watching the sun go down over the bay. I recall at one time Kevin opened up a small room serving teas and cakes to visitors. Kevin also worked for many years as a foreman with Sligo County Council, repairing roads and no doubt entertaining colleagues with more yarns.

Kevin's 'wonts' in life were few. He lived a simple life with his wife Mary and only child Gerard. Then tragedy struck when Gerard died of motor neurone disease at the age of forty-six. Kevin never really got over his death, which was then compounded by the loss of his wife Mary who died some years later. Kevin never lost the spark for telling stories, but in the end I feel he lost the will to live. I visited him whenever I was back, the last occasion being about six months before he met his Maker. I was always intrigued by Kevin's huge collection of black-rimmed memorial cards dating back to the 1950s that lay untouched in a cupboard by his windowsill. I would have known most of those people but now I have forgotten what they looked like. Their blurry photo snaps on the faded cards immediately gave them recognition. Kevin was well aware of my interest in the memorial

My maternal grandmother (Granny Kate) with her children, Kevin, May, Kathleen, Nancy and Vera

cards and, with many hints dropped along the way, his only utterance was, 'Henry, you can have them when I go.' Kevin died just before his eighty-ninth birthday in 2014, to be reunited with his wife and beloved son Gerard. His likes will never be seen again. My brother John, who inherited Kevin's house, granted me my wish and gave me the cards (thank you, John). They are now back in Oxford at rest by my armchair and, much to Sally's despair, thumbed regularly.

My uncle Peter, who was the youngest of the Keoghs, went to Birmingham at a very young age to seek employment. Peter, who has a lovely family of girls and one son, Joseph, played a part in my life when I first arrived in England. (More on that later.)

My Auntie May lives in Maidenhead with her second husband Henry. May's first husband, Paddy Davey, who also came from Sligo, died much too young and is buried in Maidenhead. I recall Granny Kate and my mother coming over for the funeral. May raised a fine family of boys and girls who are all dotted around the Maidenhead area.

Auntie Kathleen lived in Sligo town and married a man named Carty. They had a large family, whom I never got to know. Similarly, Auntie Vera lived in Sligo, where she still resides. She was married to Seanie Conlon who, again, died very young. Vera had a large family and their oldest son Eugene is a fine musician who played the pipes at uncle Kevin's funeral.

Auntie Rosie raised a family in Ireland and then settled in London after her marriage ended. I was aware of this for years whilst I was in the police and tried to trace her, but to no avail. Incredibly, she and her partner had a pub in Slough which I once visited on police enquiries. Little did I know at the time, Auntie Rosie was the landlady.

I eventually met Auntie Rosie when we bumped into each other at a funeral which was also attended by her mother, Granny Kate. You can imagine the shock on the faces of both mother and daughter when they saw one another for the first time in decades. We then saw Auntie Rosie and her family a number of times; I was pleased she saw her mother and some of my family before she died.

Chapter Two

LIFE ON THE FARM

May you always have
walls for the winds,
a roof for the rain,
tea beside the fire,
laughter to cheer you,
those you love near you,
and all your heart might desire.
(Trad. Irish Blessing)

THE FARM HOUSE

Ireland in the post-Second World War years was full of thousands of small thatched farm cottages dotted like sheep across an emerald green landscape. These houses and their surrounding farmland were set within hamlets and villages where quiet roads stretched for miles surrounded by an unspoilt landscape. The tiny hamlet of Cloonkeen in Cliffoney, where I was brought up and lived for the first twenty years of my life, was no different.

Our road followed a relatively straight line for just over a mile from one crossroads to the other, and the farmhouse where we lived sat roughly in the middle. The house was set slightly back from the road bordered by fields on either side, and I would often spend time gazing out of our front window at the Dartry Mountains, which dominated the landscape. This mountain range was perpetually fascinating to me, ever changing at different times of the day depending on the direction and force of the elements. In no time at all the clear peaks and sunlit crags would be swallowed up as the swirling mist descended in from the coast. On clear days, across the road and above a tall hedgerow, the old bog road could be clearly seen running its straight course up to Ben Wisken mountain, which was sheer and easy to distinguish with its scar-like crack down its middle. Looking further in the distance I would stare to admire the iconic tabletop mountain of Ben Bulben.

Looking to the back of our house, fields sloped steadily downwards towards the giant and treacherous Atlantic Ocean. On the horizon across the lush green valley we enjoyed a clear view of the fine and imposing Classiebawn Castle, which dominated the rugged landscape for miles.

My early memories of the farmhouse and its structure are still clear in my mind. It had a thatched roof with no felt, which made it susceptible to letting in the rain. What's more, the wooden windows were cold and draughty. The floor of the house was constructed of concrete and at times was painted different colours. It had three rooms: a kitchen/diner/sitting room with a bedroom on either side. The hearth fire in the kitchen was huge and the only source of heat; when not lit, it also provided an access point for hailstones. To the rear of the house was a stable block for the horses, and cow byres where the cattle were kept in the winter-time. There were also other stone built sheds, as big as the house itself, for housing the hens and farm machinery. Behind the sheds stood an impressive stack of turf which had been cut from the nearby bog; it never seemed to diminish in size.

The house was surrounded by tall trees, which provided a haven for wildlife and, much more importantly, a shelter from strong and prevailing winds. My father and older members of the family were wise people and did not have the 'open plan living' that is evident today. They were more interested in preventing the roof on the bungalow from blowing off.

The late 1950s saw the thatch removed from the house and replaced with sheets of white asbestos by my uncle Pat and Michael.

They burned the old thatch in the field behind the house. I'm not quite sure why it was removed, only presume it had perished and was out of favour due to the availability of cheaper materials. Nowadays a thatched roof is seen as a home for the privileged, but back then it was most likely the home of a poor farmer. Our thatched cottage blended seamlessly with its natural surroundings and was a picture postcard to look at.

I remember the thatcher, a well-respected man from the village, who worked mainly on his own. He would begin his work by laying the straw across the eaves, then overlapping as he went along the top of the house. He would then come down from the roof and start another row. Finally, the finished roof had to be secured against the prevailing winds and rain. Each bundle of thatch was either held down with straw ropes or pinned down with pointed pieces of wood. I recall this as if it were only yesterday, and was sorry to see the old thatch disappear. A good thatcher was worth his weight in gold as birds, not to mention hens, would fly up on the roof and pull at the straw for nesting material.

I seem to remember we had very little in the way of furniture, beyond a table and a few chairs; however, I do remember the dresser, where the cups and plates were nicely arranged on the shelves. Nancy seemed to have a place for everything and everything was in its place. The old radio (or wireless as it was then called) was as big as a television set and was seen as part of the furniture. It was perched on a shelf, sharing space with a few stray books and a bible. Along with newspapers, it provided the only link with the outside world. In our home the wireless was off-limits to the younger members of the family and was only turned on for the news, weather forecast and the odd football (Gaelic, not soccer) game. At the time I didn't appreciate the full impact of the news or it was discreetly kept from me. Nowadays, sadly, we've become immune to bad news; there was very little of it in my time, thank God.

In those early days we had no running water or sewage system, and toilet facilities were pretty primitive, with a hole down the bottom of the garden. Most of the houses at this time did not have the luxury of flush toilets; a chamber pot in the bedrooms was all that was available. I can remember being bathed in a wooden tub in front of the fragrant turf fire, under a dusty papal blessing. The water was supplied from boiling kettles that hung over the open hearth from what was called a crook.

Lighting up the house was a real problem in our area at the time. Electricity as we know it today simply did not feature in the days of my youth. Consequently, we used paraffin oil to service the few lamps in the house. With no electricity, washing clothes was all done by hand. What's more, ironing could only be carried out if there was a hot fire at which to heat the iron.

Cooking was done over the fire too; I can still picture potatoes being boiled in their skins and vegetables simmered in the adjacent black pot. An old black kettle with a narrow curved spout hung from the hook above. A range would arrive some years later, which was sheer luxury for cooking.

It was in the kitchen – mind you there was nowhere else to go – that the family spent most winter evenings. Life seemed to revolve around the big fire, which was never completely extinguished, and where important matters were discussed. As you looked out the front window, the presence of snow on the mountain top or frost on the hills nearby always seemed to make the fire burn cosier and brighter. It made sense to me to sit around the fire as, when the embers were close to dying out, I could look up the chimney on a bright winter's night and view the stars whilst listening to my father's hair-raising ghost stories that scared the life out of me. Looking back, I feel that those of us who were growing up in post-war rural Ireland were perhaps the last generation to hear stories around the turf fire on cold winter nights. The old thatched farmhouses are a rare sight these days, the blazing turf fires have all but burnt out, and the voices of the old storytellers have long been silent.

There is an old Irish saying, 'wide is the door of the little cottage', which was certainly true where we lived. Ours was always a busy

'Rambling' neighbours, Jimmy Mullaney and Margaret McGovern

house. In addition to us permanent residents, there was the steady stream of folk always popping in to have a chat. Neighbours would visit in the evenings and tune in to the radio to hear the news and weather forecast, which was very important to us given how much farming is dependent on the elements. I often listened with delight to the debate and repartee that took place between Michael and the rambling crowd in our kitchen by the turf fire. I remember there was always great excitement when a couple of my father's friends, Andrew McGowan and Charlie Gilmartin, came by. They would shuffle up to the warm fire and slowly make themselves comfortable on the long bench seat. The sound of rustling in their pockets would be followed by their large hands producing a bag of sweets, all lovely shapes and colours, which we savoured as we settled down to enjoy them. Every house was a rambling house like ours where the front doors would be left open. In the process, you learned the social graces and how to converse with neighbours and strangers, something which helped me in later life. Like a lot of villages at the time, local characters were very much part of the scene and were such fun to be around. I believe my time saw the best of them in my uncle Kevin, Gandhi Wymbs, Johnny Wallace, Packie Harrison and Pat McGloin, to name just a few.

Home entertainment when I was a child was simple: storytelling, cards, music and song. In the days before television you made your own entertainment, and playing cards was a particularly popular past time enjoyed by all. On most Saturday nights the card players would assemble in our kitchen, crowding around a small table. In preparation for the evening's activities, Nancy would spend the day baking currant bread and washing the best china. I was never allowed to participate in the game as arguments would inevitably result in certain players shouting at each other and thumping the table. I'm pleased to say that nothing has changed – to this day I still enjoy my card games and, yes, shouting, thumping tables and abuse are very much part of the enjoyment. In fact, shin pads and gum shields would come in handy at times!

Growing up in Ireland in the 1950s and 1960s was a far cry from today's world of computers and big money. We lived in a small farmhouse, and I shared a room with my four brothers whilst the girls slept behind a partition wall. Despite the hardship, our house was made comfortable by sheer hard work and a lot of love. Ours was

My siblings, Pat, Thomas, Joan and Pete

always a home of warmth, good grub and an open door to anyone. Yes, our family were poor, but we were no different to others – that's just the way it was.

NANCY

My mother, Nancy, was a most industrious woman; she was always doing something. In fact, I always felt she looked happiest when she was busy. Morning would see her applying brasso to her door knobs and other silverware. When she sat down, there would be a knitting needle in each hand. Like all woman at that time, she kept the house, cooked, cleaned, sewed and saw to her husband's and children's needs. She had an abundance of energy, which was made more remarkable considering she suffered with her health and was on death's door on more than one occasion.

Hospitality was Nancy's forte: she'd feed and entertain the neighbourhood without ever counting the cost, and her homemade bread, cakes, tarts and scones would be devoured in an instant by family and neighbours alike. She would bake at least six cartwheels of bread every day, placing them on the outside window ledges to cool down. Many a time a stray dog would come along and devour one or more of them, much to her annoyance. She made her own butter and had a ready supply of fresh milk, as well as selling some to the nearby creamery. In the summer the ditches carried a mass of blackberries, which she put to good use making jam and blackberry puddings.

Nancy was a great woman for making us have meals together when we came home from school – easy then, no television, or all of today's gadgets. She would make the most delicious meals from little meat but plenty of vegetables, which were grown in the nearby fields. Our diet then was traditional, with enough spuds to feed an army, although I recall they had to be cooked right as father wanted them floury and not watery. The whole family would sit down to eat, with all of us enjoying lots of salt and butter on our praties (spuds) as well as helping ourselves to plenty of sugar in the tea. The Irish are famous, of course, for being heavy tea drinkers; however, in those days we didn't have tea bags, our brew having to be strained in order to get the leaves out. Milk was never in short supply and was drunk virtually straight from the cows. It all tasted great, except the strange tasting buttermilk (the leftovers from making the butter), which I could never stand.

Although the food tasted wonderful and the spuds were piled high, dinnertime could be fraught; indeed I often wondered where the money came from to keep us all watered and fed. There were so many of us (including my parents there were seven of us before I'd even reached my tenth birthday!), enough to occupy every inch of space around the table, and if you didn't devour the food quickly enough, you were in serious danger of losing it to someone else. Being the eldest and biggest child, I had status, which gave me the advantage, I'm ashamed to say, to pinch some food from my siblings when they weren't looking.

Despite these misdemeanours, I was a thin child and people were always trying to fatten me up. Any time I went to a neighbour's house, a mug of milk was put in front of me alongside a wedge of bread big enough to feed those gathered at the meeting of the loaves and fishes without any need for a miracle. When it came to food, neighbours could actually be quite inquisitive, using it as a way of establishing 'status' within the local community. Nancy was well aware of this and, being a very proud woman, always ensured that we were all well versed in saying the right thing. If a neighbour asked what I had eaten for breakfast I was to tell them I had feasted on duck eggs, four slices of bacon, black pudding and four sausages; the latter being the Donnelly's variety and not Denny's, as Donnelly's were the more expensive brand. All slightly exaggerated of course in an attempt to show the family in a more positive light. I recall very well one neighbour commenting, 'My Henry, what a feast. And with there being so many of you ... sure your dear mother is a remarkable woman.'

Everyone loved Nancy, she would do anything, or nearly anything, for a laugh. Her magnetism attracted people, but she had a sting in the tail if you crossed her or said anything bad about the family. She would kill for us. Discipline was strict and she had to be obeyed at all costs. If you crossed over the border of acceptability you were for the high jump. I remember once she purchased a huge pair of oversized boots for me. I later found out it was to stop me running away from her. Nancy was not the same as Michael in temperament, a short telling off and a good leathering was the order of the day from her.

Outside of the house, Nancy loved spending time in her garden, and filled it with roses, gladioli, dahlias, sweet william, daffodils and tulips. April time was particularly beautiful when the fields were ablaze with rhododendrons. In contrast, Michael was not into flowers or scenery, and many a time I heard him say, 'Mam, you can't eat the scenery or flowers!'

MICHAEL AND THE FARM

Farming was in Michael's blood, but even more so in his heart. He loved his farm, looking after the cattle, pigs and horses. In the spring time, newly-born calves would arrive, a time of great excitement for us children, but days and nights of anxious waiting by Michael to ensure their safe arrival and the continuation of a healthy livestock. The winter time was the hardest on my father as all the cattle had to be brought in from the fields due to the severe weather. During the day time, he would release the cows into the fields to allow the cow byres to be cleaned by fork and shovel. Before the cows were brought back, he would lay down straw for them, then tether each of them individually by the neck to a post in their own little area. All very cosy indeed.

Michael worked hard on the land and we were self-sufficient when it came to food on the table. I remember that some of the land was poor and swampy; consequently, whatever few shillings were earned were immediately pumped back into the land with fertilisers in an

Our farmhouse

effort to improve its quality. Michael was very meticulous in his planning and would spend days preparing machinery for the different farming tasks; followed by days and weeks more of ploughing, and mowing or sowing the crop across a wide stretch of farm land. He would encourage us children to help him with lots of the different tasks on the farm and I would enjoy some, but not all, of the work. Unlike some of my brothers, I was just not as keen on the sheer hard labour involved in maintaining a farm. According to Michael, in later years my brothers Pete and Pat were the best workers around the farm. They were both as hard as nails and coped well with all the physical work. Most farm work at the time was manual and strong arms and shoulders were testimony to the constant use of the spade, shovel and fork.

Although slight in build, Michael belied his stature by carrying out heavy physical work and never moaning about the task in hand. When I was young he ploughed with the horses, which was time consuming and heavy work. No twelve furrow ploughs in those days – I remember he had one furrow and the work would take days of sweat and hard labour. Although he had a quiet disposition, Michael could be equally strong willed, especially when it came to maintaining his farm and getting the right price for his cattle. The market day would see him at his best: patiently preparing for the day, selecting the best cattle and calves to be sold; quietly making the long journey on foot to the market, and then, as the day went on, showing a steely determination to stand his ground and only accept the best price.

When returning from the market or from working all day on the farm, Michael would tuck into a hearty meal and then often sit quietly in the corner of the room smoking his pipe. He would be the picture of satisfaction under his flat cap as the haze of smoke marred his gaze and swept around the kitchen. Later in the evening he would sit by the turf fire and have us transfixed with all kinds of haunting tales. My father was a champion for telling ghost stories and many an hour was spent listening to tales of headless men roaming the area late at night, howling like wolves. He would take great delight in telling us the location of haunted houses in the village, which I would listen to with baited breath. The stories were really frightening and afterwards us children would creep to bed listening out for howling sounds and searching for shadows of headless men. At times the rain would pour down and rattle the window frames and the gates outside, creating an eerie feeling. In addition, the ceiling boards creaked and the community of little critters living in the thatch roof would erupt, putting the fear of God into you. For weeks afterwards we wouldn't dare go out in the dark on our own or go near any of the said houses. Of course, I chuckle to myself now when I think back to those times, as I'm sure the stories were told with a view to keeping us children in at night and away from mischief. Well Michael, God bless you, if that was your intention it certainly worked!

FARM LIVESTOCK

In those early years of my childhood, Michael kept a wide range of livestock, and I distinctly recall the sight and sound of dozens of hens running around the yard. We kept a sizeable number: I reckon there must have been at least fifty. Each evening they were called together and locked up to safeguard them from roaming foxes. There were many different breeds. Amongst the most popular were Rhode Island Reds, which brought a lovely touch of colour to complement the lush green landscape. Their lively cackling was, of course, very much part of the sound track of rural Ireland in those days.

I clearly remember on one occasion Nancy giving my younger brother, Pat, and myself instructions to clean out the hen shed, a job neither of us relished due to the 'pong' of hen droppings. I had the onerous task of delivering the nasty stuff to Pat from inside the shed, for him to then move it to a nearby pit. The fork was two pronged and in my hands a weapon of destruction. I'm not sure how it happened, but Pat caught the full force of a prong which entered his wrist and exited the other side. He was quite young at the time, but never cried, and we never told mother as she would have killed me. Looking back now, imagine the bacteria that entered his flesh! No jab of antibiotics then, you just had to grin and bear it.

On another occasion, I had contracted ringworm, a highly infectious fungal disease, on my left leg. Cattle were the carriers and would dispatch the spores when scratching themselves on the stone walls around the farm. It was a red ring-shaped rash, which was sore and itchy. I never told anyone about it until inflammation spread all over my leg. Nancy took one look and sent me to the doctor. The doctor got this pot of what looked like yellow paint and brushed it over the leg. After a minute the substance soaked through, leaving a deep burning sensation, and causing me to scream out in agony. I had this treatment every day for a week and had to endure the same pain every time. As a permanent reminder of this experience, the indent scars are still clearly visible on my leg.

There were few things nicer on the farm than the crowing of the big red rooster on a long hot summer's day, his calls carrying far and wide. The thought of the hens still evokes a kind of nostalgia in me, which came to fruition some years back when I let loose twenty-four

Rhode Island Reds in my back garden in Oxford much to the dismay of the neighbours. Why I didn't just buy half a dozen I'll never know. Hens running amok in a field in Ireland (no need to clip their wings in Cloonkeen) is a far cry from a small suburban garden. I got a wide awaking one morning and not from the crowing of the rooster, just frantic neighbours trying to get the hens out of their flowerbeds and vegetable gardens!

Looking back to my childhood on the farm, I clearly remember the pigs, of which probably two a year were slaughtered by a local man. The bacon was cured and smoked, hanging over the fireplace and then stored in tea chests. The flavour still lingers in my mind. This meat kept us in supply for a good part of the year. The pigs were fed on waste food like peelings from potatoes, cabbage stumps and turnips. Being pigs, they ate every morsel. To add to the fine assortment of animals and birds, we also had an ass and a couple of horses. I will always remember our white horse, a lovely animal, and would you believe it, I never, ever, got on its back.

I'm not sure how many cows we had but, suffice to say, when the Government Cattle Inspector did his annual count, a number of them suddenly disappeared. You see, the fewer cows you had the more money you got from the government. Nancy was always left to charm the Inspector with her count, which was a lot less than we actually had, and by God could she do it.

As a young boy, I enjoyed milking the cows, and singing my heart out at the same time. You see, the byres had great acoustics, which made me sound much better than I really was. I loved singing, often using Nancy's hairbrush as a pretend mic, and believed at the time I was going to be the Irish Elvis Presley. Bless her, I think Nancy thought so too as she liked Elvis and always enjoyed my impressions. Michael, however, preferred the old Irish songs. He would tell me to shut up whenever I was performing as I was giving him a headache.

Milking the cows was an art form in itself and was fraught with danger as their temperaments were unpredictable. To make matters worse, I had this awkward homemade stool to sit on, which fell over

My siblings, Mary and Pete

more than it stood up on the uneven floor. One of the hazards of milking was the ever-present risk of a swipe in the face from the cow's tail, worse still if they had been eating fresh green grass. Before milking I washed the cow's udder with soapy water to keep the milk clean and to soften the teats to release the milk. Nancy would hand me the bucket and then the fun started.

Trying to get the milk safely from udder to bucket involved squeezing and pulling the teat at the same time. This was fine, until the cow decided to throw a kick, landing you and the bucket arse over tit on the floor. My sister Mary, bless her, was afraid of all living creatures, and the large milking cow was no exception. Despite this, my fine tenor voice echoing all over the yard would alert her to the byre, where she would join me in song. Mary would find comfort in stroking the cow when I was milking. Of course, Henry was always on his worst behaviour when given an audience. I would explain to Mary that the more she'd rub the cow's belly the more milk the teats would produce. In her haste, she'd peep down at the cow's udder, only to receive a couple of squirts in the eye. Away she'd run whinging to Nancy, who would suddenly appear with a broom handle to batter me.

Although milk didn't feature that much on our farm, or on those of our neighbours, we would send at least a couple of creamery cans of milk each day to nearby Ballintrillick creamery. These cans could hold gallons of the white stuff, and would be loaded onto the horse and cart of a neighbour, Josie McSharry. Many a time I jumped on the back with Josie and emptied the milk into the machines that turned the milk into butter. It was great to experience this regular ritual.

To the front of the farm house, I would traipse the green hilly fields from one to another in search of mushrooms. Within minutes the bucket was full; in fact, they were so plentiful you could hear fresh ones rising from the ground as I pulled them up. I'd arrive home and stick a dozen or more on a long thin metal skewer on top of the turf fire, each one filled to the brim with salt. The greatest difficulty was trying to prevent the lovely juice from dripping into the fire and spitting onto your face as you awaited the special treat. They were all mine and sharing was not an issue. To this very day, I simply love mushrooms.

I earlier recalled memories of my father on market day choosing the best cows to be sold. Market day, or 'fair day' as it was called in my time, was certainly one of my favourite times of the year. After breakfast Michael and I would go in search of the livestock he had selected to be taken to the fair. After a few forays into different fields, we would gather them up ready for the off. The nearest market was about six miles away, so you can imagine a herd of cows chasing along the roads, entering every field that didn't have a gate. You could hear the lowing of the cattle from a distance as other farmers had taken the same route. It was a twelve-hour day. A price was asked for and a counter offer made, which was always refused during the earlier part of the sale. Then the haggling would start, when open hands were spat on and deals made towards the end of the day. This type of haggling and hand slapping seemed to me to be a well-rehearsed script, which in a way I suppose it was. It was not unusual to stand all day waiting for an offer, which would eventually arrive after more hand slapping and arguments. From this, I learned how to wheel and deal to get bargains. Some of the cows would not be sold and had to take the same hazardous route back home again. Michael always had a little drink to celebrate if he had had a successful day, much to the anger of Nancy who was waiting for him to return with the money.

This type of fair day is now a thing of the past, relegated to the pages of history.

A Blessing for Fair Day
God be with them now,
and bring them home
with their fair share
of stock or money.
(Trad. Irish proverb)

I recall our horses were regularly shod in the village at the blacksmith's forge. There were, in fact, two forges, which were owned by the Hannons, two bachelor brothers. The forge was a busy place and a hive of activity, with men waiting their turn to have their horses shod. I would hazard a guess and say they were the busiest of all the tradesmen as the horse was the mainstay of farming at the time. They also made all their own tools before mass production flooded the world with factory-made steel and iron products. Both of the Hannon brothers were village born and bred, and classed as good at their trade.

They were powerfully built men with strong sinewy hands like shovels and many a day during school holidays I would spend in their company. Winter evenings were my favourite time to visit, when the cold outside would cut through to the bone … but the glow and heat from the furnace would warm the cockles of your heart.

Heating the iron in the furnace at a very high temperature with the use of powerful bellows was the key to turning the metal on the anvil to any shape the smithy required. I would stand around to watch this fascinating work. First the removal of the old shoe, the paring of the hoof, the first fitting of the red hot new shoe, the beating on the anvil, the cooling in the tub of water and the clouds of steam, the final fitting of the horse shoe with the square headed nails, and the finishing gloss of the hoofs with shiny black paint.

Sadly, the forges are no more and the smithies long gone to their place of rest in the sky.

LIVING OFF THE LAND

Spring time was a busy time of year for the whole family with the preparation and sowing of vegetable seeds and potatoes; I enjoyed helping Michael with the planting. The land was always dug by horse and plough, and then came the back-breaking task of sowing the potatoes, which were the staple food for each meal for the rest of the year. As the weeks went on, the potato stalks appeared out of the ground, and then the spraying would take place. A large barrel filled with water was transported to the potato field by horse and cart, and then a bag of powder was added which turned it a lovely sea blue. Michael would then fill the large sprayer with the blue mixture, put it up on his back and walk up and down the rows spraying the stalks to prevent the blight from destroying the crop. At any one time this could be a quarter of an acre of spraying – no easy job. This work obviously didn't do me any harm as these days I am now the proud grower of vegetables in my own allotment, helped by grandson Danny who, I jokingly remind, is officially in charge of the cow dung.

Of all the chores on the farm, thinning turnips was the most detested. In fact, at the time I would have described it as the most boring job in the world. Michael would announce to the assembled bodies around the dinner table that the turnips were ready to thin. Rain was needed to soften the ground which made the work a fraction easier but, despite Nancy expecting me as a farmer's son to be straining at the leash to contribute, muddy earth did not appeal to me. The strongest and largest plant had to be left, extracting the weaker ones to the dustbin. The fingers suffered as there was no way of protecting them from the elements, mind you stinging nettles between the rows did the trick of warming them up.

Despite rabbits becoming a commodity and saleable to local hotels and restaurants in later years, they were looked upon as a nuisance as they could do a lot of damage to the crops if their numbers were allowed to multiply. To keep them under control, Michael would do a cull, setting traps and snares in the appropriate places. Another technique was to use a ferret to go down the rabbit hole while placing a bag over another exit point; the rabbit would then pop out straight into the bag. I was always wary of the ferret, having been told they would climb up inside your trouser leg and bite your 'mickey'. As strange as it may sound, I recall seeing locals with pairs of rabbits on the handlebars of their bicycles on their way to mass.

I had a fascination for the open air from childhood, with a firm belief that no roof, however big, was as grand or as beautiful as the sky above. Therefore, of all the activities I looked forward to during the long summer break, my favourite was being part of the hay making team. The hayfields had different names, like 'the big fields' or 'the wet fields' – no need to explain any further.

Michael sensed when the grass was ripe to cut, and most of the work was done manually by rake and fork, if you did not have your own machinery. We were lucky as Michael had a horse-drawn mowing machine with a seat on it that cut the grass in swaths, which would then be left to dry. He would spend days preparing by sharpening the blades and oiling the machine, a ritual all on its own. When the grass was cut you left it a day to dry and then turned it with a fork to dry it on the other side. Sounds fun; however, to save six or seven acres was extremely hard work. Before the machine it had to be cut with a hand scythe. Sometimes you had to shake the grass to remove any moisture out of it. The number of times this was done depended on the weather, as a good, dry sunny spell was essential.

The radio played a vital role in determining when the weather was good enough to commence the work. Once the grass or hay had dried out, it was then ready to rake into small piles or lappings and built into tram-cocks. These were the long dome-shaped round towers of hay that were such a familiar sight in the fields at that time. It was normal for someone to stand on top to trample it down (subject to 'hurricane Debbie' not taking you on an unexpected flight forty miles north!) whilst Michael would fork it to you; absolutely back breaking even for a fit teenager. Plenty of sweat and elbow grease were the order of the day, but it was clean work and we liked being out in the fields. I particularly enjoyed trying to leap over the tram-cocks or kicking a ball between them. My poor dad was tired of showing me the correct way as it was 'in one ear and out the other', as he would say. When the hay was stacked it had to be secured using thick twine. Some weeks later the haycocks were removed by a large flatbed trailer to the garden next to the house, where they would be built into a huge haystack called a rick. Once the hard work in the meadow was over the place would become a hive of activity, with the neighbours joining in and helping to construct the enormous rick. This was a reciprocal practice amongst farmers. Meanwhile, Nancy would be busy cooking and supplying dinners to all the workers.

Come harvest time we would all help out with a variety of tasks, including gathering the potatoes, turnips and other vegetables from the fields, as well as 'stooking' oats, which involved gathering bundles of corn which had been cut by Michael with the hay machine. This was a tedious enough job as each bundle was tied together with string and then left leaning upright with others so that they all supported each other. They were then left to dry and ripen until the big day when the threshing machine arrived, which separated the grain from the straw. Michael hired out the threshing machine (or thrashing machine as we used to call it) from a local man who toured the countryside with the machine when it did its annual round in Cliffoney each autumn. It was a huge piece of machinery and, if my mind serves me correctly, was driven by traction using a large rubber belt. The machine would sift the corn from the sheaves before emerging from the back to be poured into bags already placed on pulleys – in doing so it saved a lot of time and hard work. Once full, they were lifted off and replaced with new bags. The corn would then be sold and the straw used in the winter for animal bedding. A couple of us had the unenviable job of standing on top to throw the bundles of straw into the machine. This was a particularly dangerous task as, if you slipped, it was 'high noon' for you. I also remember the dust cloud from the machine was awful and would cause irritation to the eyes and throat. There was no time to feel sorry for yourself, though, as you had to work at the speed of the machine, which ate up the sheaves of straw in a flash. Our pace of work was also kept in check by the knowledge that Michael was paying for the hire of the machine and so was keen to keep things moving at a fast pace! Similar to haymaking, the process of harvesting was a communal affair, with neighbours helping each other out. The setting would be a buzz of noise and activity, with even the cats and dogs joining in as they chased the rats that scurried from underneath the mounds of straw.

In those days there was no public water supply in our area, in fact no running water of any kind. We had to rely on the river and streams to provide water for washing and feeding the cattle. We complained about the long hike to the well for a bucket of drinking water but we all had to take our turn. The enamel bucket was heavy when empty, let alone full, when it cut the fingers off you. We did not have our own well on the farm despite many valiant attempts by a water diviner to locate one.

The water diviner walked the fields with a bamboo-like cane, which would bend and point towards a spot in the ground where he believed the spring water would gush up. Michael would spend days digging a very deep hole, only to discover brown bog water. I've seen this happen on many occasions and doubted this method of finding water. There were two wells in the townland, one in neighbour Tommy Haran's field and the other much further away. Michael got permission to use them both.

Looking back, over half a century later, walking to the well was brilliant exercise and quite therapeutic. The field where the well was located would see cattle grazing or lying down peacefully. Given that my sister Mary was afraid of the cattle, she was excused from the job. You see, cows are very nosey and will come over to you to investigate what's going on, which would cause Mary to run a mile.

The nearest well to us was entered by climbing over a stone wall and then a couple of steps down to fetch the water. This water was used for drinking, cooking or making tea, though the sight of a frog leaping out of the well could be a bit off-putting! Rainwater from barrels outside the house, captured by drainpipes from the roof, was used for other purposes. Well water, according to folklore, was good for you and very healthy. It also contained properties which were cures for various ailments. Nowadays, of course, it is constantly filtered and checked for impurities, before being sold on.

THE IRISH BOG

Getting a stack of turf home from the bog for the winter fuel was a must for the family when I was young. Our bog land was about two or three miles away from our home and was passed down the generations from family to family. You may ask where the bog is derived from. Well, it was established from areas where forests were cleared when the climate was warmer. The roots would rot down to make the land very wet and swampy.

With the passage of time it's difficult to pick out special moments as a child, but lighting a fire and boiling the old metal kettle on the cinders at the bog was a real treat for me. We would also boil eggs and have a tasty meal during the turf cutting. My fascination at the time would have been sitting by the fire and watching the flames, and listening to the chat of all the other men with Michael.

As I got older I was expected to take an active part in stacking the turf once they had dried out. I was never allowed to cut the turf, a tough physical job which required a great deal of stamina and strength, as I was no good at it, thank God. The top layer of heather had to be stripped or cleaned; sometimes it was burned off. The bank, as it was called, usually five layers deep, would then be cut using a special spade. This was followed by the turf being handled individually with great care. Once dry, the turves were then constructed into little clamps ready to be taken home.

My father, by his stack of turf

The heat in the bog, which rose up mirage-like, was intense. Nancy would always smother us with her own concoction of sun cream, which was always needed on a hot day or you would get burned. The aroma from the fluffy white-headed bog cotton was everywhere as it blew idly in the breeze, and in the evening, still hot and humid, the midges tormented us and ate us alive.

Another fun part of this work was loading the turf onto the cart and holding the reins of the horse on the way home. Days would be spent bringing the turf home piled high and expertly built to withstand the friction of the cart wheels on the old roads. By the time the last cart was filled the novelty had worn off and there was no trace of yours truly.

I remember my father would always wear a cap and, when greeting people along the road, he would take it off to show respect. Many families with common surnames would use all their first names to identify which family they belonged to. One man who I believe was related to us was John Terry Billy Connolly. Michael would always address him with the words, 'good morning, John Terry Billy'. Strange now, but true!

There was no modern machinery in my time and, consequently, there was a time when you would see hundreds of people on the bog with as many fires smoking up the sky. However, as Ireland prospered in the 1980s this way of working ended and the government placed a ban on turf cutting to preserve the landscape for future generations. In recent times, with a down-turn in Ireland's economy, the bog is back, but now the work is carried out, in the main, by huge machines that travel on caterpillar tracks. My own brother Pat prefers to cut the turf by hand as he enjoys manual work. (Much to the despair of his wife, Sheila, who has turf stacked to last a lifetime.)

The bog land has for centuries been, and continues to be, a vital energy source to Ireland. In these changing times, with modern machinery now making older methods of working the land redundant, I'm pleased that my sons and some of the grandchildren have had a chance to spend some time working in the bog land, using the original tools and catching a small glimpse of what it was like for me and my ancestors all those years ago.

Our people of the 1950s and 1960s were predominantly rooted in an agricultural world barely recognisable from the Ireland of today. Farm life was a physically demanding existence aided by simple tools and machinery, but just as importantly by a strong community and a spirit of togetherness. Michael had to work hard as money only came in when we sold cattle, potatoes or other agricultural produce.

Growing up in the village, I took the green fields and trees for granted and didn't wrinkle my nose at the inevitable farming smells. Every year, like heralds announcing spring, the daffodils bloomed together with the profusion of primroses that grew in wild abandon on the laneways and in front of an old house nearby. Sadly, with advanced methods of farming, many of those wonderful little flowers have now disappeared.

I learned a lot from my days on the farm, from feeding the animals, milking the cows, saving hay, stooking oats, spreading turf and the whole process of sowing and reaping. It was lovely to have witnessed the milk being churned into butter as well as the spinning wheel making wool. I was so used to country life, from the singing of the birds in the spring and summer to the harsh chill winds and rains of winter. In fact, life on the farm was busy all year round. Bored? We never knew the meaning of the word!

CHRISTMAS

As a child, I loved Christmas. For me it was the most magical time of the year, when we were off school and listened to the radio blaring out 'Rudolf the Red Nosed Reindeer'.

I will always treasure my childhood days when we were all together gearing up for the big day. What irritates me most nowadays is to hear Christmas adverts and see decorations in the shops before the witches and pumpkins have appeared.

My memories take me back over sixty years to the event that heralded the approach of Christmas for us: walking the bog roads and seeing the red berries on the holly bush. In preparation, the turkey would be hanging upside down from the high rafters of the horse stable so that the dog or cats could not reach it. Nancy had no trouble in killing a turkey for our Christmas dinner, which would have been arranged weeks beforehand.

Bright red and silver paper decorations adorned the ceiling and the windows and, to my excitement, I would be allowed to put the freshly cut holly on top of the pictures and along the picture rail. Most Christmas cards were placed on a piece of string and hung from the same picture rail as the holly, with some getting pride of place alongside a picture of the Pope and the Virgin Mary. Sometimes Michael would procure an evergreen tree from the nearby woods, which would be tastefully decorated with silver paper and small toys.

No matter how often my teachers and parents spoke of the nativity, I never ceased to be enthralled by the crib which Nancy so carefully put together with the holy family and animals. It took its pride of place on the big windowsill in the kitchen.

This was a very special time for the children, when Radio Eireann would enthral us with a visit to the North Pole to witness Santa Claus leaving with his presents for all of us. (When I was young, I actually believed that all the people talking lived inside the wireless!)

All of a sudden it was Christmas Eve, cold and frosty, with snow covering the top half of the mountain (snow at Christmas is rare these days but was often seen when I was young). The kitchen floor was scrubbed early in the morning, and Michael would sweep the chimney to allow Santa to climb down, whilst reminding us that good children would be rewarded and bold ones would be deprived. The letters had been written long ago to Santa in the hope he would deliver the goodies we wanted. The household would be all abuzz

My siblings, Thomas, Pat, Joan (back) and John (front)

with preparations for the big day, including the arrival of the festive food and goodies from the local shop. Nancy was now preoccupied preparing the turkey, stuffing and vegetables (I don't ever recall Michael helping out in the kitchen). The smells of cinnamon and spices filled the kitchen.

Early evening and it was my job to light the large red candle on each windowsill, ensuring they were placed well away from the curtains. This was called the Christmas Candle, a beacon to lost souls. They shone brightly and gave the house a warm glow from the outside. Michael would then appear with a bottle of holy water and sprinkle it around the house and soak all the children in his excitement. Come eleven-thirty, Michael and Nancy would mount their bicycles and head for Midnight Mass, leaving me in charge to steep the peas and keep an eye on the trifle to ensure it was setting properly (no fridge or freezer then). Before leaving, Nancy would warn me not to keep dipping my grubby little finger in to taste it every few seconds. In fact by the time they got home there was half of it missing!

By now all the younger children were sound asleep in bed, waiting for Santa to arrive. Nancy would advise us to go to sleep quickly as Santa was a shy man and quite apt to make a hasty retreat should he discover that children were still awake. It was the only night when we would voluntarily go to bed early. Most of us had arranged our stockings on chairs by the chimney, mistakenly believing that the bigger it was the more we were likely to receive. Because our house was so small, myself, and my brothers, Pete, Pat and Thomas, would share the one bed, two at each end. The bed bowed in the middle, meaning the youngest, Thomas, had the misfortune of being crushed by the rest of us (no doubt affecting him in later life). The bedroom was warm and cosy as we cuddled up under the bedclothes.

By six o'clock in the morning, the house was in complete disarray, me trying to get a tune out of the mouth organ kindly given to me by Santa for good behaviour and kindness all year round (here was a man hard of hearing and with poor eyesight). The others were popping up in the beds and grappling for their stockings in the dark. Oh, the sheer excitement of finding a toy gun, an orange and a few sweets in the bottom of the stocking. Being the eldest, Santa might just leave me a large spud, which caused uproar with the others; other times a pair of boots; he even went to the bother of putting steel tips on the heels and studs on the soles. Our wishes were simple, and I never recall Santa disappointing us.

We might have a piece of toast or a boiled egg for breakfast, then I would hit the road running for the eleven-thirty Mass. Outside, dozens of bicyclists leaned precariously against the walls of the church, with people talking and discussing the rights and wrongs of Christmas. The few cars parked outside were black, with long bonnets. Inside the church, the altar was decked with flowers and holly, and a large Christmas tree stood on the sanctuary, nicely decorated against the fragrant smell of candle grease and the glow from the red candles. The church was heaving, seats full of worshippers, all in their best attire. Then I would kneel down, say a silent prayer by the crib, followed by a tear in my eye when the choir sang 'Silent Night'. Peace, perfect peace.

The day itself was usually peaceful too, with the children playing with their toys. Work on the farm was kept to a minimum, although the cows still had to be milked, and animals and poultry fed. About two o'clock, Nancy would give a loud shout and call us for dinner. There was then a stampede into the kitchen, all screaming 'I want a leg'. I clearly remember Nancy's words, 'eat what you are given and shut up'. The table was covered with a nice colourful tablecloth and was laid out beautifully, with neatly placed cups for the lovely red lemonade, a rare concession and a very special treat. Nancy dished out the grub – turkey, floury spuds, cabbage and turnips. Her flavoured stuffing and gravy was worth dying for. No one could touch Nancy when it came to making gravy. Then the plum puddings and trifle would arrive, followed by more red lemonade for the kids. Michael would have a bottle of porter.

After dinner the rest of the day was spent playing in the woods or in the fields. Fresh air was the answer to Nancy's prayers when we would disappear to give her some peace and quiet. We only had a radio in the house, television was in the distant future, but despite the lack of these latter day recreational essentials, the day passed all too quickly. Christmas over! We were shattered, but there was always next year.

> *The magic of Christmas lingers on,*
> *Though childhood days have passed,*
> *Upon the common round of life,*
> *A holy spell is cast.*
>
> (Celtic verse)

Chapter Three

RURAL VILLAGE LIFE

THE LAND OF HEART'S DESIRE

Few Irish towns have a more beautiful setting than Sligo, and you can understand why the poet William Butler Yeats called it 'The Land of Heart's Desire'. The landscape is stunningly beautiful, and it was a magical place to grow up in as a child.

Surrounded by the mystical and magnificent Dartry Mountains, in my younger days there was no better way for us to experience this mountainous landscape than to explore the Glencliff Horseshoe, so called because of its shape and layout. About four miles from Cliffoney, this single-track route around the Dartry mountain range gives close up views of Ben Whisken, Tievebaun and Truskmore. The scene around the Horseshoe overlooking Sligo and Donegal Bay provides some of the most beautiful views in Ireland: its green slopes, embroidered with myriad white sheep, dominates the skyline. The ruins of the old schoolhouse still stands as testament to this once populous valley.

Whilst walking or cycling around the Horseshoe I would marvel at the dramatic cliffs, which were full of mystery; indeed, one such cliff was said to contain the cave that served as a hiding place for the mythical runaway lovers Diarmuid and Grainne. My mate John Barry's ancestor's old homestead was a place nearby that we used to visit, and climbing the steep slopes was always a challenge we looked forward to. Nestling at the entrance to the Horseshoe in the hamlet of Ballintrillick stood the creamery, which, apart from turning milk into butter, was also the focal point for people to meet and discuss the topics of the day. I understand from my grandchildren that this type of forum still exists – it's called Facebook. My, how things have changed.

The coastline surrounding Cliffoney is equally mystical and charming to me. The beautiful white strand of Cliffoney beach is only accessible by walking along an area known as The Borough, then climbing over the sand dunes onto the beach below. The rip tide currents are particularly strong and, according to locals, the sea is too dangerous to swim in. In fact, I recall in my childhood years a swimmer getting into difficulties and drowning there. It's such a shame as the coastline is by far the loveliest in the area.

The jewel in the crown of this unique countryside is without question the little seaside resort of Mullaghmore, with its rocky cliffs defying the Atlantic gales. Its picturesque harbour and wild sweep of the ocean is beautiful. A vast expanse of golden sand unfolds to the front of high sand dunes. To walk the head of Mullaghmore and see fishermen perched precariously on the black rocks in touching distance of the knife edge cliffs and the snarling waves was, and still

Mullaghmore Head

is, quite breathtaking. When it comes to Cliffoney and Mullaghmore, the lyrics of Frank Sinatra say it all: '*you can't have one without the other.*'

Situated about two miles from Cliffoney, I would spend many weekends during my childhood walking around Mullaghmore, taking in the atmosphere of the place, especially during the summer months, when the area would be thronged with holidaymakers and visitors from across the isle, particularly Northern Ireland.

Unlike Cliffoney beach, it is safe to swim at Mullaghmore. Despite this, it's incredible, looking back at all the time spent there, that I never learned to swim until I came to England. The old saying, 'the nearer the church, the further from God', rings true.

VILLAGE LIFE

Away from the coastline, mountains and home life on the farm at Cloonkeen, village life as I grew up was vibrant and played an important part in my upbringing. Situated at either side of the crossroads leading towards Mullaghmore, St Molaise's Roman Catholic church and

Cliffoney village in the 1940s. My grandfather Henry's sister, Ann-Jane Higgins, is pictured (front left) outside her house. Clancy's pub and Harrison's are pictured left; village post office to right

Cliffoney national school would both feature prominently in my life. Also within close proximity at the time stood several shops, public houses, a local doctor's surgery, a post office, the village hall and the Garda station, all of which hold very special memories for me.

One of the most vivid memories of my childhood is of being dispatched to the village shop by Nancy aged about nine to buy the family's groceries for the weekend. Winter provided that cosy feeling as I wandered the roads wrapped up to the neck with a heavy coat and Nancy's knitted gloves. I had a list as long as your arm and no money. You see, the shopkeeper allowed time to pay; it was called getting provisions 'on tick'. Michael would go down every fortnight and settle the bill.

The farming community were well catered for at a time when travel to the big towns was difficult. There were three main shops in Cliffoney. McGowan's was situated along the Sligo to Bundoran road about a mile from the village. It was very much a general store which stocked everything from groceries to animal food. It was an Aladdin's cave. You could get all you needed to serve every stage of your life, from towelling nappies and huge safety pins to a wooden box to take you out of this world, and everything in between. This reminds me of my daughter-in-law, Alison, coming home from Aldi recently: she went for some sausages for lunch and came home with wet suits (made in Japan) for my grandsons Harry and Archie.

To the front and very close to the main road stood the only petrol station in the area, as well as an undertaker's business. The petrol pumps were manually operated by cranking up the pump handle to and fro, and the shop had a long wooden counter, behind which the owner Tom Gardiner sat in a small kiosk doing the books. He came out occasionally to check what was going on.

Timoney's was more of a grocery shop. It stood the opposite side of the church, and was run by a brother and sister. The shop had a shed situated to its left where I would bring a large wet radio battery to be charged up overnight at a cost of ten shillings. I then had to carry it back with a promise from Michael or Nancy that I could experiment with the dial and tune into some more radio stations. Cissie, the owner, was hidden away in a dome-like kiosk behind the counter and would appear as soon as you entered the store. They were generous people who never forgot their customers at Christmas; the arrival of a box of goodies was greeted with delight.

Charlie McCannon's shop was opposite the school. On opening the shop door, you would hear a bell echoing along the long corridor to his living quarters. Then, his footsteps and a faint light from a candle to greet you. A most sociable man, who was always in good humour, Charlie had the shelves in the shop constantly stacked with empty boxes to give the impression the shop was full of stock. I would visit there once a week to get Nancy her green box of asthma powder (which gave her some relief for her breathing), Michael's tobacco and an ounce of snuff for one of the elderly neighbours.

Meanwhile, back at the farm house we would all await weekly visits from two local shopkeepers, who would stock up their vans and drive around the local community selling a variety of items. At the time, travelling shops provided a vital service to rural areas which had little or no means of transport. The advent of cars and public transport were the death knell of this service. (Of course, things have now gone full circle and the 'travelling shop' is now a delivery from a big supermarket as a result of ordering groceries on the computer!)

First there was Jack Davey's large blue van packed with 'goodies' which would announce its arrival every Wednesday evening by a hoot of the horn. There would follow the excitement and mad rush to the back of the van where Jack would sit observing every move in case you took something without paying. He always wore a long dark overcoat, even on the hottest day of the year. The other visit was from the local butcher, Paddy Burns, a real character who is still hale and hearty and well into his nineties as I write this. His van would pull into the front of the house every Saturday evening when there was a big hug for Nancy. Despite his powers of persuasion – Paddy could sell sand to the Arabs – Nancy was never fooled, and her choice of words would scare the living daylights out of you. If Paddy had sold her meat the previous week with too much fat or gristle on it he'd be told about it in no uncertain terms. So much so, many a time I saw the van roaring off at speed, with Nancy threatening him with the broom handle. What a woman!

The Garda station was located in the village and, as I recall, had four officers. Now it begs the question: why in the 1950s and early 1960s, at a time of very little or no crime, did it take a sergeant and two to three Garda to patrol the village? I seem to remember, the Garda's role back then was to sign dole and benefit forms, issue summonses if you were caught riding your bike without lights or keeping a dog without a licence, and check for the illegal brew, poteen.

As for the local doctor, at a time of very few women in the higher echelons of public or private life, a lady doctor had her own practice in the heart of the village. A formidable woman, she was not the friendliest of people, and you had to be at death's door to pay her a visit. I had this dubious honour when I received a nasty cut over my eye which needed stitching. The doctor's rear garden backed onto the school playing field, resulting in footballs being kicked into her prize garden. She would never return them to the school; you had to be either brave or daft to fetch it back. I wasn't brave but would jump through the hedge in an endeavour to get the ball. Not for a second did I think she ever saw me retrieving the ball, but as the good doctor was inserting the last stitch over my eye, she said, 'if I ever see you in my garden again, you will need stitches over the other eye'. I got the message!

I believe sometime in the middle of the last century a crochet school was opened in Cliffoney. I'm not sure of its first location, but it was certainly in business as I grew up. The business was run from a property belonging to a dentist on the main road and, at the time, employed quite a few people.

And then there was the post office, which in those days was run by the post mistress, Kathleen Clancy. When I think of all the post office's ancient equipment, it's similar to that shown in American films. Two postmen were employed, covering miles on their bicycles, and at

Christmas time a part-time worker would assist. Telegrams were in huge demand, at times relaying messages of bad news – maybe the death of a loved one in another country. Kathleen was privy to the contents of all telegrams. Very few people had phones in this era – it was pre-mobile phones, text and twitter and, as the postman went about his work on foot and bicycle, the only twitter around was that of the birds in the country hedges and fields. To make a phone call via the post office was a complicated and expensive business, with the postmistress directing operations behind a high counter. You could just about see the top of her head if you were lucky.

There were five public houses in the village when I was young and all brought with them their own hub of excitement, and funny stories aplenty.

Hannon's was the largest pub and stood at the crossroads just outside the village. It had its own small brewery and corkage licence (the labels on its bottles were stamped with Hannon's Brewery). Next was Cummins', which was a frequent watering hole for the mass goers, who would queue outside on a Sunday morning until it opened its doors. Along the road from there was Dunleavy's, which was run by Owen Dunleavy, who combined the pub life with a bit of farming.

Harrison's had been a family pub from the beginning of the last century and when I was young it was run by Michael Harrison. Michael was a great Sligo Rovers soccer fan and many a time took me to the show grounds in Sligo to watch his beloved team. Here was a real gentleman who was a sound businessman too; I remember him adding a small grocery shop to the pub. I have memories to share about working behind the bar in my early teens, but more of that later.

And lastly Clancy's, which in my youth was more of a spit and sawdust pub. The bar was very small, but generated a terrific atmosphere amongst the customers. There seemed to be a palpable sense of history when its genial host, Hugh Clancy, set about pouring pints of porter

Michael Harrison (left) with a customer outside his pub

from his own homemade distillery, or at least that's the way it looked to me. I recall many sayings originating from the four walls of Clancy's, such as the land being so fertile that knitting needles could be grown on it, and men being so mean they would steal the milk from your tea if you weren't looking. Wise words indeed. The pub was popular with visitors, especially at weekends, when the local characters would arrive late, having already had a skinful in one of the other pubs.

On one occasion Hugh became aware that a bus load of holidaymakers from Scotland were due to arrive in the area with the intention of visiting the pub. Now, good news for Hugh, but with one small problem: such was the primitive state of the pub, there were no real toilet facilities. Something had to be done and quickly at that, so Hugh set about finding a car tyre to place over a bucket for woman to sit on as a loo. Days later, after numerous complaints, some of the woman returned enquiring about the best way to remove tyre print from their arses. Hard to believe, but a true story!

CLIFFONEY NATIONAL SCHOOL

Clasping Nancy's hand as a five-year-old down a long winding road on my first day at school was my earliest recollection of Cliffoney National School. The school was built in 1914 during civil unrest in Ireland. I remember as we entered the main road, which by today's standards had little or no traffic on it, several boys and girls cycled past us. It was a daunting day. Squeals of delight resounded as children greeted each other after the long summer break. I was crying as I tightened the grip on Nancy's hand, and wanted to go home.

It is often said that your school days are the best days of your life, but in truth I never liked school and to me it was an unnecessary evil. Running down the road, skirting pot holes, school bag bound with a leather strap hanging off my shoulder, the only thing I looked forward to was playing sport and the laughs with friends at break times or when walking home.

During lunch break, we sometimes played throw ball with a bundle made up of rolled newspaper and held together with string. Marbles (or taws) was also a popular game which could be heart-breaking as you could lose all your taws to a bigger lad. Alternatively, we went out to the big field behind the school with a tennis ball, charging about like young calves let out to fresh grass, with coats for goalposts.

Cliffoney national school class in the late 1950s (me far right, back row; my sister Mary, third from left, middle row; my cousin P.J., second from right, front row)

Of course you don't see kids going to school barefoot anymore, but when money was scarce the majority of the kids went to school without shoes in the summer.

I remember having cuts and bruises to my feet and in the real hot weather I would arrive home with tar stuck to the soles of my feet. This didn't go down well with Nancy.

Likewise, very few people owned cars back then and walking to school was the norm. As I got older, I could walk my way blindfolded to school, I knew every twist, turn and bump along the way on my mile journey.

As well as the school bag, the other thing we had to take to school each day during the winter was a sod of turf. Our classroom had an open fire in the corner and all the pupils had to supply the turf to keep it burning. The classrooms had individual wooden desks with ink wells to the front for pupils to dip their nib pens into. Sometimes the ink would spill out over my copy book, which resulted in big blots obliterating what I had written, which was always a good excuse for me to hide my poor work!

The teachers did their best; however, if there was a school curriculum of any kind I certainly wasn't aware of it. As for left-handed pupils, they were forced to use their right hand at all times, and were punished for not doing so. I recall that one lad had a stammer which, as you can imagine, was not helped by the constant abuse from the rest of us.

I didn't have a care in the world until I entered the school gate and was bombarded with rules of all sorts. Discipline was strict and the teachers didn't spare the stick – their motto being 'spare the rod and spoil the child'. Can you imagine this treatment nowadays? I endured all amount of slaps with the cane with no outward expression of pain. It was not the proper thing to display any sign of weakness or cry. Many a slap I got from the teachers for whistling. One of them even called me the 'phantom whistler'. I suppose it was a comfort thing and a way of me engaging with the rest of the pupils. I also tried yodelling at school – and more caning was my reward.

There were times, of course, when my behaviour probably did warrant a good telling off. One example I can think of was the way my friends and I used to entertain ourselves when there had been snowfall. I loved to see the snow on the ground and, during mischievous moments, my friends and I would take turns to wee in it. I recall coming a cropper many a time when trying to write my name, but struggled on reaching the 'y' of Henry. Doubling back on yourself under such circumstances is not a good idea!

Another big attraction to me at the time was an orchard of apple trees in the priest's grounds. Apples then were as scarce as hen's teeth, so I often joined a band of assassins that raided the orchard, testing the ripening fruit and then using some of them as hurling balls. My bad behaviour of pinching the apples came, however, with a price. I obviously ate too many at one time and became violently sick afterwards. It served me right. Ever since I have been unable to eat a raw apple, though my mother's apple tarts were a different proposition. No doubt the good priest found out and put a curse on me.

As I got older I recall walking home with a mate of mine looking for jam jars, either digging them up in fields or finding them in backyards. You see, the local grocery shop would give you one penny for the large jar and a half penny for the small one-pound jar. This was a lot of money in my time and it would pay for us to see the cowboy films at the local cinema in Bundoran. The singing cowboys Gene Autry and Roy Rogers were my favourites. They were marvellous times with Gene and Roy starring in the old black and white films. I recall that we watched the films through a haze of grey smoke as many of the boys and girls smoked Woodbines throughout the performance. On top of that the grainy pictures were awful and the sound quality was poor (hardly a high-definition experience), but boy did we love them.

Education was simple in those days, with an emphasis on the three R's, religious studies and the Irish language. At the age of about fourteen, shortly after leaving primary school, I recall going to Rosmuc, an Irish-speaking area in Co. Galway, for a month to learn more about the (*Gaeilge*) Irish. I'm pretty sure I had to pass an exam for entry. It was a real eye opener, as nobody in the village spoke English and Irish was the everyday language. To survive you had no choice but to speak it. I enjoyed the experience and took in all that was best in rich Irish heritage, culture and folklore. It was a shame I never had any need to use it in later life.

Maths and English didn't really interest me – like a lot of kids I was more passionate about sport and music; indeed if there had been a subject at school on Irish song lyrics I'm sure I would have topped the class. Outside of school I absorbed music as much as I could, whether hearing songs over the wireless or occasionally hearing a live musician such as Pat McGloin, a local character who played his melodeon (a type of accordion), or Peter Mullaney on the fiddle at different events. Like most Irish counties, Sligo has generated a wealth of songs over the years. I suppose the better known ones include 'Down by the Sally Gardens' and 'The Isle of Innisfree', both from the pen of William Butler Yeats. On leaving primary school, I knew more about the lyrics of these types of songs than I did the times tables. Thinking back, another unusual passion of mine at the time was learning parrot fashion the name and diocese of each bishop in Ireland. Over time I gathered an encyclopaedic knowledge and could recite all the popes covering the last century. What a pity I didn't absorb mainstream subjects in the same fashion. Funnily enough, my own son, Duncan, developed similar traits when growing up. I recall him learning off by heart every football FA Cup winner. I guess it's a Wymbs thing!

I never lost my fascination with the Vatican and years later, on a visit to the eternal city, we visited St Peter's Basilica and of course I couldn't wait to see the tombs of the popes. Unfortunately they were only allowing members of the clergy down to the crypt ... so on a whim I turned my collar round to join the queue.

I got my just desserts, however, when, after an hour, I surfaced (by a different route) to see no trace of Sally or the other members of our party. With no phone and not even the name of our hotel, I was in a right pickle. Having wandered around Rome with no sense of direction and no understanding of any Italian, I was, to say the least, utterly lost, so you can imagine how over the moon I was when I caught sight of a face I recognised and was reunited with our group. I must say the papal tombs detour was worth it though!

Looking back, I was never aware of any great hardship whilst at primary school. Academically I did okay and left at fourteen with my primary certificate. At the time of leaving, the head teacher told me I had brains to burn but wouldn't use them. Not sure whether or not he was talking to the right pupil.

CHURCH LIFE

In many ways, my early life – like others around me – was dominated by religion, and its practice and observance of rituals. I received my first Holy Communion at the age of seven and confirmation a couple of years later in 1955, when I was given the name Kevin to go with Henry Joseph.

The build-up to receiving the sacrament of Holy Communion was an intense process. Weeks beforehand the catechism had to be read and learned, and the local priest would test you on its readings and decide, with your teacher, if you were up to the required standard. Soon we were rolling these godly phrases off our innocent tongues, not having a clue what the heck we were talking about. It was also an expensive time for the family as a new suit and black shoes were purchased for the occasion. As a memento of the day, Granny Kate took mother and myself to town and bought me a solid silver medal with my name engraved on the back. At the time it cost nineteen shillings, a fortune then, when the average weekly wage was five pounds. I still have the medal to this day.

Following Holy Communion I was an altar boy for a good many

Me as an altar boy, aged 9 years

years and by the time I extinguished the candles for the last time I was into my teens. St Molaise's Roman Catholic church around 1956 was my date with destiny when I wore the mass-server's outfit for the first time, along with a pair of shiny black shoes. The mass server garments were called a soutane and surplice. It was like an apprenticeship and I accepted my lowly position relatively well. Some of the duties were really testing, like lighting the highest giant candles. Until fully trained, a server would shadow a senior altar boy. In my time, the mass was in Latin and you had to be fully conversant in translation and communication. As altar boys we saw up close every ceremony and sacrament. I witnessed the joy in the eyes of many a bride and groom, together with the tears on the faces of bereaved families at funerals.

Ringing the bell at the appropriate time during mass had to be precise. I remember one day I knocked the church bell over and woke up half the congregation. The missions[1] were another time when the church played a key role in the community. Dozens of tents would be erected outside the church, each one full to the brim with religious medals, rosary beads and the like. The assembled clergy were the original fire and brimstone merchants, shouting and bashing their hands on the pulpit, everyone damned in hell if they didn't conform. As I got older my responsibilities grew and I was appointed the bell ringer at the church. This involved a set procedure of ringing the large bell outside at midday and at 6pm, Monday to Friday, for the Angelus. It was heard miles away, and observed by everyone, who would make a sign of the cross and prayed for the dead. This practice continues today and is still observed on national radio in Ireland.

Confessions were a topic no one talked about apart from the children. In the confessional box, you were not supposed to be identified to the priest, when he would ask the standard question 'have you committed any sins since your last confession?' I always had the same list to confess: telling lies figured prominently, along with being disobedient to Nancy. At no time did I confess to pinching the priest's apples. The penance was normally five 'Hail Mary's and an 'Our Father'.

I would sit very close to the box to say my prayers and also in an effort to hear what others were up to. I remember a few occasions when someone who was hard of hearing entered the confessional and would shout out loud to the priest. The priest would know very well

---

[1] The missionaries were priests who arrived from Dublin for a weekend of prayer and devotions at a particular time of year. They were impressive looking men, wearing big long brown robes. They didn't need amplification as they could holler like bulls. They preached about the flames of hell and the devil that lurked in dark and lonely lanes. No doubt referring to courting couples. This subject seemed to occupy their minds more than other sins like dishonesty or violence. Nobody in their right mind would question them.

the people entering the confessional box. He once quietly said to me, 'you should be telling me about eating meat on a Friday'. (Friday was known as a day of abstinence when you were only allowed to eat fish.) Chance would be a fine thing – we were lucky to get it on a Sunday, never mind a Friday.

When I was growing up in the village, the church was full. On Saturday night there were queues for confessions, which was very much the norm and was taken for granted. There would be two mass services on Sunday morning. The annual missions were well attended, which ensured the fear of God was around for at least another year. A big drawback to Sundays, however, was the fact that you had to wear your best clothes.

I don't believe we were a particularly religious family, although my father Michael was slightly more devout than mother Nancy. Michael would stand in the church porch with other farmers during mass and would disappear before it ended. Nancy attended when she could but was often prevented by ill health. It was very much going through the motions. I remember the campaign for the family rosary[2], with Michael telling us that 'the family that prays together, stays together'. For us young children, this just degenerated into fits of giggling.

Of all the influential people who lived in the village, the parish priest certainly held the 'high' ground. Here was a man who lived in a large two-storey house in its own grounds of about fifteen acres, and benefited from a resident housekeeper who looked after his every need. He was very much a priest of the people who visited the school frequently. I saw lots of him over the years when I would ring the Angelus bell. It's quite extraordinary to think that now there is just one priest to cover three churches in the area, which in my time had

---

[2]   The rosary is a well-known recital of prayers in the Roman Catholic Church and is a form of meditation to Mary about the mysteries of joy and sorrow. It still forms a huge part in funerals and church services.

two parish priests and two curates. In later years, I learned more about the priest. He had a great and abiding love for the songs and music of Ireland. Before he died, he was made a canon (the next step up from parish priest) and is buried in the chapel grounds.

In some parts of rural Ireland, the local priest continues to do a round, twice a year, visiting every area of their parish. They stop off at a house in each station area[3], allowing the faithful to hear mass and receive the sacraments. This event is held before the two great Christian festivals of Easter and Christmas. The mass takes place on a rotating basis and is a long-established custom in most parts of Ireland and still continues today in our area.

Due to only occurring once or twice in your lifetime, it made the whole build-up very exciting. This was a big event for my family as you were opening up your house to all and sundry. For Nancy and Michael it was time to decorate the house inside and out in preparation for the big day. I remember Nancy did the whitewashing outside as she didn't trust me with the brush. She feared that, out of laziness, I would cut corners and opt to paint around any bicycles leaning against the gable wall instead of moving them, as well as get more paint on myself than on the walls.

All the neighbours would take their turn to stage this event. The best china and cutlery were used with the priest sat at the top table. The kitchen would be used for the mass. I remember ours wasn't big enough and people stayed outside to listen to the priest.

After mass was the big feed for breakfast and then the collections when the heads of each household went up to the priest and placed their offering on his plate. No wonder I had thoughts of becoming a priest when I left primary school! It frightens me now to think how much money was spent to organise this mass as we didn't exactly have a pot of surplus cash to throw around.

There was always an abundance of quality food, drink and cigarettes,

---

[3] The stations as they were called were a 'blessing' of the houses in the village to ward off spirits, disease etc.

and I know of one bachelor farmer who opted to have the station mass said in church to save expense. The story goes that when the arrangements for the stations were being announced the angry curate said, 'Ah we'll have to get a wife for him'.

TRADITIONS AND FESTIVITIES

The Irish were very much into traditions when I was young – and still are today – many rituals being part of folklore.

Take funerals: today they are all very dignified affairs. When I was young there were no funeral parlours and the corpse was laid out in the person's house. A death in Cliffoney was a big occasion involving the entire village and beyond, and it brought work to a halt in the immediate area. The bereaved family was visited, respects were paid to the corpse and the wake got under way. A man's life was judged by the numbers attending the funeral (although the weather could affect the turnout).

From my experience of funerals as a youth, I firmly believe we should have our funeral rituals before we die, then we would know who arrived to pay their respects and who didn't, and could treat them accordingly. Given that people invariably speak well of the dead, it would be good for the self-esteem to hear all the nice things people have to say about you.

When someone died, the priest arrived and prayed by their bedside. The body was washed and laid out on the bed in a brown habit, the front of which was decorated with a picture of the Sacred Heart. These were available from the local shop.

Pennies were sometimes put on the deceased eyes to keep them closed and removed before visitors arrived. Two lighted candles and a crucifix were placed on the white linen covered table beside the bed (the white linen was kept especially for such occasions). Shortly afterwards there would be a steady flow of people arriving to pay their respects. Tables, chairs, kettles and teapots would be carried from neighbouring houses, and a huge fire burned on the hearth over which kettles hung on the iron crook, always on the boil.

All the visitors would be saying nice things about the deceased. 'Ah sure, he looks great, the best looking corpse I've seen in years.' The most amazing thing for me was the introduction of bottles of Guinness and loose tobacco and cigarettes stacked on plates for people to help themselves. Family members would sit by the bed in an all-night vigil, and it was a custom for people to smoke clay pipes which, as a mark of respect, would be broken in half before the funeral. The following day the drone of voices saying prayers filtered from the bedroom and the large crowd in the kitchen and outside fell silent for a while.

Then the undertaker and hearse arrived with the coffin. More prayers were said and then the final goodbyes, with everyone crying. All the lights in neighbour's houses and shops were turned off along the route. Men doffed their hats and caps in respect as they stood in the roadways ready to join the cortège. Everyone walked slowly behind the hearse. The priest then met them at the chapel gates and sometimes male family members would bear the coffin into the church where it would stay until the funeral the following day.

It was usual for the family and neighbours to dig the grave (this still happens today) and it was bad luck not to throw a bottle of whiskey into the grave with the coffin. There was no such thing as the green plastic covering in those days, more's the pity, as old bones would be visible in the pile of earth. Women of the house were expected to wear black for a year after the death and music was forbidden for the same length of time.

In the case of roadside accidents, as an additional mark of respect, wayside shrines were dotted all over the place, as well as white crosses along the road indicating the spot where the person met his Maker. This is still true today.

Older people of Cliffoney strongly believed in cures and superstitions.

I remember one day I got this awful cramp in my stomach which caused Nancy some anxiety. She told me to go and see an old lady in the village who had the cure for it (no local chemists in those days). The lady advised me to spit under a large stone, say the Hail Mary and the cramp would disappear. I got home, lifted the biggest stone I could lay my hands on, spat under it and, in doing so, dropped the bloody thing on my foot. Apart from the cramp I now had a sore foot as well. No Hail Marys this time. Granny Kate's words immediately came to mind, 'Keep the faith Henry'.

Despite this experience it didn't put me off and, being a bit vain, I thought to myself, wouldn't it be nice to be able to cure people? It would make me important in the eyes of my mates. With this in mind, one day on a visit to Bundoran I picked up the courage to see a fortune teller in her caravan. This old lady with white hair greeted me with open hands.

I told her about my ambition to be a faith healer. She looked up to the sky and mumbled something. Five minutes elapsed, when she whispered, 'I predict you will soon have the cure for the burn, but first you will have to find a "man-keeper" and lick its belly three times, and say an act of contrition. This has to be witnessed by two people but not from your own family.' Fortunately for me I knew what a man-keeper looked like – a small lizard, newt-like little creature (possibly a salamander), longer than a frog, all slimy and smelly. They lived in land drains and were difficult to find.

Rather bizarrely, Nancy was over the moon on hearing the news, setting Michael the task of finding me one. I too was excited and told all my school mates. They all wanted to be witness to the big event as they didn't believe I would do it. Michael was quite a religious man in his own way and believed in cures. Nancy was more interested in telling the neighbours of her son's fame. One day Michael called me, and there it was, this awful slimy smelly little devil, bigger than I imagined, with a long body and greenish in colour. Two of the neighbours were called for, so I had no choice now but to do it. I found it difficult to hold it never mind lick its belly. Anyway I took it from Michael, turned it over, and gave it three long licks. That was that, I was now blessed with the cure and would be able to charge a fee for my services. And what has happened since then you may ask? Well, I would love to be able to say that the rest is history but, unfortunately, my special powers never came to fruition and, consequently, I never had any customers to enable me to make my fortune!

St Patrick's Day was one of the most enjoyable days of my childhood. In days leading up to the 17th March, the radio would be blasting out 'It's a Great Day for the Irish' or Bing Crosby with his touch of genius, singing, 'The Isle of Innisfree'. We were all told in school about the significance of the day. Saint Patrick, who had once been a simple shepherd, came to Ireland in the year 432 AD, a little while before my time, bringing with him Christianity and banishing the snakes.

England has its rose, Wales its leek, Scotland its thistle, and Ireland its shamrock, a symbol for the holy trinity. Nancy would make sure my hair was neatly trimmed and my shoes polished for mass, and woe betide you if you passed a derogatory remark or comment behind her back that you didn't want to go.

With a day off school, we celebrated in style. One year Nancy bought me a green suit, which was quite outrageous and embarrassing. I had to wear it for mass and of course other children were laughing at me. I was only about nine at the time. We all wore our sprigs of shamrock, which we picked from the fields or garden walls.

It was difficult to distinguish the shamrock from the clover, as they looked much the same. We also wore St Patrick's Day badges, all green and gold, putting great strain on the brand new safety pin pinched from Nancy's sewing box.

Talking about dressing up in green reminds me of a time when I was about fifteen and I enrolled for civil defence classes in Cliffoney. The classes took place all over Ireland and were in response to the ongoing cold war between America and Russia, which almost resulted in a nuclear war in the autumn of 1962 during the Cuban missile crisis. We were trained for a couple of years on how to monitor and measure the radiation level with special survey meters should a nuclear war break out. I suppose the ideas were good, but thankfully we never had to put them to use. At the time I didn't have a clue what the classes entailed and wondered why Nancy was so keen for me to join. I soon learnt that the big attraction was the pair of boots, gloves, beret, and a long green overcoat that Nancy used as an extra blanket on our beds! I believe that the Civil Defence was called the FCA. I'm not sure what the letters stand for, but we used to call it the Free Coat Association!

Anyway, back to St Patrick's Day ... Every town in Ireland made a special effort to honour St Patrick, Sligo town being no exception. According to friends that witnessed it (I tended to stay in the village) marching bands would parade and play happy tunes in Sligo. At night time, a ceili dance[4] would take place in the village hall, with young and old leaping around, swinging and enjoying themselves. Ceili dancing was very popular in houses in my youth. All you needed was someone to play the accordian and a good stone floor, which was the norm then. The good dancers would have specially prepared shoes with steel toe caps to make the floor spark when they danced reels and jigs.

St Patrick's Day is these days a truly global celebration of Ireland and all things Irish, enjoyed from Sligo to New York, Dublin to Sydney.

---

[4] This type of event is now gone, but ceili dancing is still popular in village halls where a ceili band would perform.

I recall that Bonfire night was a big event in Ireland during my childhood and celebrated on the 23rd June, its tradition originating from the pagan midsummer festival. Weeks beforehand, old tyres, wood and gorse or whin bushes were piled high by the roadside, ready to be set alight. Can you imagine the black smoke from the tyres bellowing up to the sky and the pollution it caused? As might be expected, there was plenty of eating, drinking and all night dancing, each little hamlet having their own party. Come nine o'clock, the scene was ablaze with all the locals enjoying themselves. Our music was supplied by local character Pat McGloin, who was happy to oblige with a tune on the melodeon, especially when a little alcohol was on tap for him. Prayers would be said before the bonfire was lit asking for God's blessing on the crops. It was our custom to take home a burning ember from the communal fire and place it on the family hearth for good luck. The custom still exists today, with maybe one bonfire in the neighbourhood, similar to bonfire night in England on Guy Fawkes nights.

In addition to the bonfire night summer event, each August bank holiday saw the local sports day on the village green in Mullaghmore, when we witnessed the best in swimming competitions from the pier, athletics, in which I won quite a lot of silverware, bicycle racing and football. What's more, the tic-tac men took bets on the likely winner of the Donkey Derby race, which leads me to a funny story.

One year, when I was about fifteen, I was asked to ride one of the donkeys (called Sligo Lad) as its regular rider hadn't turned up. I'd never been on any animal's back before, indeed I struggled to ride me bike without falling off. Now what I didn't know at the time was my donkey had previously won this race and was firm favourite with the bookies. To the starting line and disaster, the donkey wouldn't move. All he kept doing was throwing his hind legs up in the air and farting. Every effort was made to coax the stubborn mule, including a good walloping from the owner, but it was no good. In short, the ass would not move its arse! Those who had put money on him were not best pleased and needless to say yours truly got the blame. My Donkey Derby days were thankfully numbered. Funnily enough there's an old Irish proverb: 'the world would not make a racehorse of a donkey'. I couldn't agree more heartily!

CLIFFONEY VILLAGE HALL

Popular music played a prominent part in my life, despite my having little exposure to it as a child. The old Irish songs I grew up with taught us more about our history than many of us learnt from our school books; however, youngsters wanted to move away from this style of music. Dancing then was set to an old time waltz where you would see older folk take to the floor. In my teens, the music scene in Ireland was in a transitional period. Popular music was emerging, despite conservative opposition. Irish national radio introduced some programmes in which presenters played the new chart material, such as Elvis, Buddy Holly and many acts emanating from America and the UK. Change was slow to come locally and live bands only made an odd appearance in the area; however, things were changing and the young natives were getting restless.

Around about 1961, a folk revival was sweeping across America, as the Clancy Brothers and Tommy Makem, together with Bob Dylan, were making inroads into the American and Irish music scene. The Clancys and Makem were from Ireland and had sparked a rebirth of Irish traditional music as never seen before (the Clancy Brothers in particular were a huge influence on future Irish stars; without them we may never have heard of the Dubliners or the Fureys). They always sang those rowdy, raucous songs focusing on themes such as immigration, drinking, rebellion and brawling. I loved listening to their music, and my friends and I tried to imitate them. The Clancys were famed for their white woolly Aran jumpers, which meant every mother and grandmother in Ireland at the time were soon putting their knitting skills to good use. We all wore them and, bless her, Nancy had to knit more than one for me. When dirty, which was

Me in my itchy Aran sweater (mid-1960s)

most of the time, I would steep it in a basin of water only to discover it had shrunk, leaving poor Nancy to take pity on me and knit another one. As well as the jumpers shrinking, I seem to recall I wore them without anything underneath, and suffered from the itchy wool on my bare skin. Years later, whilst at the BBC, I was fortunate enough to interview the older of the Clancy brothers shortly before he died and still have the recording on an old reel-to-reel tape. What a privilege.

Dancing was a popular pastime during this period and Cliffoney Village Hall was the only venue available for people in the area. As an emerging country, with electricity not present in every hall, the facilities were pretty basic, with the bands running their amplification from large batteries. Nonetheless it was a very exciting time.

The big event of the year was the Christmas Parish Ball, when a well-known dance band would perform. This was allowed on a Saturday night to raise funds for the church. On the day of the dance local committee members would visit houses collecting pre-prepared food and milk. Come the evening, I would be down at the hall peeping through the windows.

Teenagers were not allowed in under any circumstances; however, as the evening progressed, it got busy and an opportunity would present itself. I'd move swiftly behind someone's back and spend the rest of the evening backstage listening to the band. Sometimes band members would feel sorry for me and bring me tea and sandwiches. I remember getting caught on one occasion by a woman committee member who promptly told the priest. He came looking for me but I hid under the stage for ages. I had to face him the following day at Mass and he gave me a strong lecture about staying out late at night. For goodness sake, I was fifteen at the time and the dance had finished by half eleven!

The clergy held enormous power over the people. More importantly, they ran many of the dance halls, including Cliffoney Village Hall. The priest would patrol the dance floor and even separate couples that were deemed to be dancing too close. They would also inspect the grounds surrounding the dance hall to ensure that couples were not getting too familiar (chance would be fine thing). In the eyes of a teenager, it was spoiling the opportunity for a kiss and a cuddle; however, in the eyes of the church, it was ensuring that sins were not committed.

Sunday night was the big night for dancing. Saturday night was frowned upon by the church authorities; so much so, 'no dancing' was insisted upon as people had to get up for Mass on Sunday morning. Never mind having to get up for work on Monday, this was irrelevant in the eyes of the church. In addition to the annual Christmas Ball, a monthly dance 'hop' would take place. I recall hearing that one lady remarked to the priest, 'I don't like your balls very much, but enjoy your hops'.

The power of the priest and the church was absolute. It is evident that many of the church teachings were very good, but in the entertainment world it had something of a stifling effect. The church strictly enforced a ban on all dancing during the seven-week period of Lent from Ash Wednesday to Easter Sunday, the only exception being St Patrick's night on the 17th March. During this time bands would cross the pond to tour in Scotland and England.

The hall was also the focal point for various other activities, like concerts and meetings. It was there that I had my first dance (and a refusal to dance) at one of the monthly 'hops'. It was also the first time I ever saw the girls at one side of the hall and the men at the other. More on that later.

I remember on one occasion, I was about fifteen at the time, and had obviously consumed quite a substantial amount of drink (red lemonade), when I picked up the courage to ask a girl to dance. She took one look at me and said, 'I'm not dancing with you, you are too young to be out on your own and as for that awful shave lotion ...' I was annoyed as it showed me up in front of my mates. I was quick in response and said to her 'I like your hairdo, did you knit it yourself?'

Anyway, to my surprise, this other girl took pity on me, walked across, promptly grabbed my hand and asked me to dance. At the time it seemed more like an order than a request and I didn't have the heart to tell her I had two left feet and couldn't dance at all. On reflection I probably didn't want to appear more of a prat than I already looked!

Chapter Four

PART-TIME WORK AND PANEL BEATING

THE VOCATIONAL SCHOOL

After Cliffoney school, my life saw a big change when I joined the vocational school or 'tech' as it was called. I'm sure everyone can remember that period in their life when they are coming of age, that feeling of freedom and excitement for what might lie ahead. For me I now look back with great fondness at the close friendships I forged then. Although life was not always a bed of roses, and school was to be endured rather than enjoyed, there were plenty of enjoyable and funny moments along the way.

The vocational school system was an unhurried scene with a great emphasis on trades, commerce, rural science and home economics. In theory, it prepared you for the job markets in these areas, which at the time covered most propects. I soon came to realise, however, that who you knew was better than what you knew. The 'cute hoors' (aka slippery customers) at every turn in Irish society looked after their own, politicians being at the forefront with their fairy tales of how school leavers would find good jobs in Ireland. I remember one of the teachers advising me to try and improve my education, although it wasn't everything, he said. A little story he related to me at the time is still engrained in my brain. To suceed in life, you need some luck and also drive, to push hard for what you want. He then pointed to

ARBOR DAY · 1962

A happy looking group of students prepare to bring shelterbelts to their own homes for planting in 1962. Front row (L-R): C. Blayney; T. Herity; B. Carway; M. McSharry; R. Drury; M. Mannion; M. Currid; J. Gallagher; H. Reynolds; P. Hargadon. 2nd Row: M. Henry; I. Feeney; S.A. Watters; M. Herity (Ardtrasna); M. Carway; E. Barber; M. McGowan; H. Rodgers; B. Kennedy; M. Barber; I. Stewart; (?-?); M. Gallagher. 3rd Row: S. Barry; (?-?); S. McGowan; L. McDaniel; B. Coleman; O. Herity; H. Gallagher; J. Warren; L. Devins; J. Watters; S. Feeney; H. Wymbs; J. Feeney; P.J. Gallagher; P. Watters. Back row: K. Mannion; F. Smyth; T. Gillen; J. McElroy; T. Currid; A. Warren; (?-?); J. Currid; M. Dwyer; (?-?); P.J. McGowan; F. McHugh; N. Haran.

the classroom door, which had 'push' on one side and 'pull' (influence) on the other. Both of those will help along the way, he told me.

My journey to the 'tech' was about five miles on an old rusty bicycle that Uncle Pat had given to me. It's fair to say that I walked as much as I cycled as the chain had this nasty habit of slipping off just as I was pedalling up a hill. Talking of bikes reminds me of a time when I borrowed Uncle Pat's bike without permission and collided with a well-oiled eejit trying to straddle his bike on the road. I managed to buckle the front wheel and handlebars and Nancy felt awful about this and ran me to the shop to get bread and butter to make sandwiches... I suppose she wanted to butter him up with sweet talk and sandwiches to get his mind of his buckled bike. Anyway, on the way back I went rambling into my friend, Terence, leaving the loaf of bread outside. Half an hour later I found the chewed remains of a butter wrapper and two crusts – Terence's dog 'Carlow' had eaten the lot. (The crusts were left as the dog had no teeth from catching stones we threw to him.) The next minute I met Nancy running furiously to see where I was. I stayed out of her way for the rest of the day. Uncle Pat never forgave me for this dirty deed, and always reminded me of it even when he was an old man.

Back to the tech: the vocational school had five teachers, the head being a Clare man who addressed us in Gaelic. The curriculum consisted of English, Irish, Maths, Mechanical Drawing, Rural Science, Chemistry, Physics and Woodwork. The girls would learn Bookkeeping and Cookery instead of Mechanical Drawing and Woodwork. I believe we had Religious Studies for an hour each week, when the few Protestants would go elsewhere. Being a largely Catholic community, there were as many Catholics at the 'tech' as you'd find in the Vatican.

One of the teachers gave me a belt across the head most days for misbehaving in class. He saw corporal punishment as the way forward. This teacher did most of his work from the blackboard with his back to us. There were about twenty-five in each class and being a bit of a 'Jack-the-lad', devilment was never too far from my mind. I remember making myself a catapult and spending ages mastering the art of firing pieces of chalk with real accuracy. Of course the back of his head became a legitimate target for me. He was as cunning as a fox and would wait his turn to punish me, invariably in the afternoon after I had been grassed up by someone over lunch. Knowing what was potentially in store for me, I was always on my guard and would sit towards the wall in the middle of the room well away from him. When the time was right, he would move swiftly in behind my seat and then reward me with a knuckle rap to the back of the head. Obviously with each beating, a desire for revenge set in and, despite having to face the consequences, I would take aim with my catapult at his head, ten out of ten every time. I have to say now that my behaviour was not the best.

Mechanical Drawing was another of my least favourite subjects. The teacher, took an instant dislike to me for some reason and was known to give students a kick up the backside. When the weather was reasonable the teacher would take the class to the nearby field. This particular day the field was muddy after a period of heavy rainfall. Nevertheless, out we went with our drawing boards and pens. The teacher always wore the same long white coat and I sussed he was in bad humour on the way out and stayed out of his way. However, for some reason he came in my direction and aimed a kick at my backside. Seeing it coming, I was quick enough to grab the offending leg, causing him to lose his balance and drop onto the muddy ground, covering his white coat in muck. He got up, called me a prig, and limped off to tell the headmaster. I knew I hadn't done anything wrong; I was only protecting myself from his kick. The other students got a great 'kick' out of it (excuse the pun). I was ordered home and told not to come back by the headmaster.

How was I to face Nancy? She would kill me for bringing shame on the family as I'm sure she had high hopes for me at the time. Anyway, on the way out I spoke to the caretaker who was big into football, told him what had happened, and that I was due to play in the football team the following day in an important game. I was a bit cocky at the time and I knew that this could potentially help the situation as the team needed me. He told me to hang around the garden for a while; he would have a chat to the Head. A few minutes later out comes the headmaster. He ran up to me, no mention of football, and told me in no uncertain terms to go back and apologise to the mechanical drawing teacher who was sitting down nursing his knee. I went in and apologised. By this stage the teacher was unable to move from the chair, otherwise I'm sure another kick would have ensued. I was told to report for school the following day with my boots and togs. Then matters went from bad to worse: we lost the game, and I got my marching orders for allegedly kicking an opponent. I was learning fast; my teacher would have been proud of the kick himself!

Although academically I felt I was a bit of a disappointment to my parents, I had one feather in my cap: I was a decent Gaelic footballer, which endeared me to other students. Actually, truth be known, study was something I did between football matches.

The school football field was usually my sanctuary, but at times I had to come face to face with a man who owned the adjoining field. He had a dislike of footballs being kicked into his field, and would

GRANGE V.S. FOOTBALL TEAM · 1963-'64

Grange Vocational School Football team 1963-'64. Back row (L-R): Tom Currid; P.J. Leonard; Oliver Mitchell; James McElroy; John Barry; Frank Smyth; Richard Herity; Hugh Gallagher. Front row (L-R): Jimmy Currid; Michael Currid; Henry Wymbs; Jim Heraghty; Dermot Mitchell; John Watters; Seamus Feeney; Jimmy Harte.

frequently put a sharp knife through the ball, then throw it over the fence in bits. I'm sure the teachers were scared of him and would not intervene. Like a fool, I would take him on, but at a distance, and fetch the football. He would growl and make stabbing gestures towards me. Although I knew I was able to run faster than him, I was always a bit apprehensive when leaving school in case he tried to teach me a lesson for my actions.

During my time at the 'tech', I was looked upon as a little above average scholar with a reputation for fooling around instead of paying attention. I had difficulty keeping up with maths, physics and chemistry. English was my favourite subject as well as rural science, which I particularly enjoyed as we would get out into the fields and survey the trees and insects. I also took part in amateur dramatics, usually playing the eejit, which came quite easy to me. I was told I had a fine singing voice and didn't need much encouragement to go up and sing some country song. As well as Gaelic football, I excelled at handball and I learned a fair bit about growing flowers and vegetables, as well as how to face the school bully. I managed to keep away from the fags due to my football ambitions, and alcohol was not even on my radar.

Despite the punishments, the teaching staff were generally good, with some students obtaining good jobs in the building trade and forestry commission. As for me, I carried on at school until I was about seventeen, achieving reasonable exam results (much to my surprise). With three years of vocational school behind me, I was ready to find a job, but doing what? At that stage I didn't have the foggiest idea.

GAELIC FOOTBALL

My teenage years began with a calling. Believe it or not, I felt the priesthood was my destiny. Admittedly, Granny Kate's gentle persuasion in the form of bribery money played a part in my thinking, but I was also influenced by my cousin having been ordained a priest in Dublin and by the Irish missionaries in the Far East. What's more, Nancy's monthly magazine, with a montage of Irish priest's photographs, similar to footballers at the time, also kept my interest in the priesthood alive. But then my young life was turned upside down when news spread that one of my best school friends, John Gallagher, had died before reaching his sixteenth birthday. He only lived a couple of fields away from me. It took me quite a while to get over the shock and during this time I lost interest in the idea of becoming a priest. Interestingly enough, my youngest brother later married John's niece Tracy. Small world indeed.

Deciding that the priesthood was not for me, I consumed myself in my number one passion, Gaelic football[1]. Oh how I enjoyed those teenage days kicking a ball in the fields from dawn to dusk. Gaelic football and hurling weren't just sports, they were a release from the thoughts of homework and manual work on the farm. Those were the

---

[1]   An integral part of Ireland's national heritage and a sport with ancient origins in which two competing teams of fifteen players kick or punch the ball between team members, ultimately to convey it over the opposition's crossbar (scoring one point) or into their goal net (scoring three points).

Me with my friend John Barry and Terence Leonard's dog,
Carlow (the dog with no teeth)

days of carefree discovery, and kicking a ball passed the time. It did
not matter if the ball was made simply from newspapers tied together
in a rag, as long as it provided the means for a match to be played
with gusto and the vibrancy of youth. Croke Park for me was Terence
Leonard's field near the village, in which up to thirty of us would
assemble during the summer evenings and after mass on Sundays. You
may ask why we didn't play on one of our own fields. Michael and
Nancy never stopped me, only our land was very wet and uneven and
Terence's field was more central for everyone. Play could only start
once we had shifted the cow shite off the field. We arrived dirty and
went home dirtier. The better players among us would be split up to
ensure the teams were evenly matched and not too one sided, coats
used for goal posts. The football was hard, no quarters given and none
asked for. It was thrilling stuff.

Funnily enough, hurling[2] was my first love. I even made my first
hurl from a spoke of an ass cart. I used an axe to chop it down, then
I shaped it out with a hatchet, finally finishing it off with a penknife.

---

2   Another true Irish passion: more than just a form of hockey/lacrosse played in Ireland
     ... a physical celebration of Irish ancient traditions and culture.

It took a month to design and when finished it still looked like a spoke from an ass cart. Nobody from the carpentry and joiner's guild contacted me with an award for my work.

I remember there was a big iron gate to the front of our house which in time became a target for me, where I would practice smashing a small ball with the hurl through the openings. When I attained near perfection I devised a plan to tie some net wire – not sure where that came from – to sections of the gate, making it more difficult to get a ball through, which I did on occasions.

There is no tradition of hurling in my part of Sligo, so I could only listen to the commentary on the radio. I loved the game and was in my element when Nancy bought me a real hurl in around 1959. I knew in my heart she immediately regretted this purchase. You see, our farmhouse had a large frontage, with millions of pebbles scattered all over it. Every minute of the day I would emulate famous hurlers of the time, with hurl in hand striking every pebble over the tall trees into the nearby field. I did many other things with that hurl too. I threatened my brothers, the hens, scattered flies and anything else that came within striking distance. Come springtime, the blossoming heads of daffodils and Nancy's prize tulips would be sent soaring into the air with some delightful strikes from my beloved hurl. Then, without warning, the hurl inexplicably disappeared, never to be seen again. Even to her dying day, Nancy swore she had nothing to do with its disappearance.

Now I have a garden of my own I realise the torture I put her through and have experienced the same problems with my children and now my grandchildren, who are ever ready to kick a heavy football into my prize plants and hanging baskets. I'm sure my yells are the same as I heard from Nancy long ago.

Apart from the dim memory of my first sight of the round leather object, the earliest football activity I can recall is cutting out and pasting into a scrapbook pictures from my local paper of famous Sligo footballers. Although only nine years old, I can still see the faces of those players. As I got older I became less parochial and national figures began to capture my imagination. Sadly for me, the scrapbook disappeared some forty years ago along with many of my football heroes.

There was no organised underage football in my time. We played our own game and enjoyed it, which is a far cry from the under-10, under-12 and under-14 competitions now. Similarly, there wasn't a great deal of proper coaching; I was once told when taking a free kick to use the tip of my boot when delivering it. No wonder the ball used to sail out towards the Atlantic Ocean! 'Togging out' was also done in the ditch, often in the pouring rain.

I first played competitively for the 'tech' at under-15 level. We didn't have a great team and were always knocked out at an early stage of competitions. But we did have some fine individual footballers, like Seamus Feeney, John Watters, Hugh Gallagher, Dermot Mitchell, Mickey Currid and one of the best underage players I ever saw in Tommy Currid. Gaelic football was my passion and I lived for it, so it was always difficult to come to terms with the fact that there were some better players than me!

One of my abiding memories of playing football in my youth was how heavy the jerseys were. They were made mostly from wool and were very uncomfortable and hot in the summer, whilst in winter they retained all the water and reminded me of a horse jockey carrying weights. The old leather football took some beating, with the shoelace sometimes sticking out from the inside bladder. A swipe of it across the face was worse than a splash from a cow's rear end. On a wet day the football was difficult to hold without breaking the tips of your fingers as it got extremely heavy from absorbing so much water. A scar on one of my left fingers is still there to prove it.

I was fortunate at the time, however, to have a pair of blackthorn football boots which had leather studs nailed into them. On occasions the nails would pierce the skin and a loud roar from me would echo across the field as if I had scored a goal. On other occasions the shoe lace would break and a bit of twine would be used to keep the boot on. For those without the proper footwear, I can still see an opponent slipping and sliding while playing in cut-off wellies in a game in the rain.

The only competition was the minor championship at under-18 level. I played at this level when I was sixteen and won my way into the county minor team. Even though I say it myself, this was no mean achievement for a county the size of Sligo. We had little success though, only disappointments along the way. Amalgamation then took place between three or four of the village clubs and success came at last, winning minor and junior in 1965. I'll never forget the crowd of supporters swelling the sidelines cheering us on to win. Looking back now, I was always the glory boy, never wanting to play in the backline because it meant you were the provider, rather than the player who applied the glorious finish of a goal, and inevitably got your name and maybe picture in the local rag.

Funnily enough, those trips out with the football team to nearby counties were some of the few occasions when I travelled outside of Sligo. You see, we just didn't have holidays when I was growing up in Ireland. We were no different to others at that time and, due to living close to holiday resorts, had no need to go further afield anyway.

Sligo was always the poor relation when it came to Gaelic football. Sligo town was the nerve centre for the soccer team, Sligo Rovers, and consequently the town and county were divided between soccer and Gaelic football. It was also difficult to break into the county teams if you were from Cliffoney, as the odds were stacked against you: the selectors all came from the other side of Sligo and invariably choose their own first.

I always had a great love for the seven-a-side tournament, when teams would turn up with familiar faces under different names, having packed their teams with top players from other counties. I played a lot of those games in different counties and gained valuable experience of how to look after myself. Punch ups and brawls were common practice among players and supporters. I was no saint myself and was well capable of dishing it out should the need arise.

The top seven-a-side tournament at the time was held about three miles from me in Ballintrillick. In all, about twenty teams would turn up from all the neighbouring counties, with their best footballers.

I'll always remember getting to the final with our local team, which was a tremendous achievement. The team included myself, alongside six McHugh brothers, all of whom played at county level at some stage of their careers. A huge crowd had assembled to witness a nail biting finish. With minutes to go, we were ahead when one of their players, who was much older than me, smacked me in the face. Game abandoned, with fisticuffs everywhere. The most annoying thing about it all, I never got hold of either the winners' solid silver cup or the losers silver medal.

I believe this match took place the day after England won the World Cup in 1966. I remember watching it on a tiny black and white television screen in Clancy's pub, whilst enjoying a bottle of coke.

Gaelic football meant everything to me in those days and to be selected for the county team was something that one dreamed about. It was a source of great pride and fulfilment. I continued playing football at a reasonably high level until I left Ireland in 1968.

THE SHOWBANDS

In the early 1960s we still didn't have many ways of listening to music and, due to a shortage of radio stations playing pop music, Radio Luxembourg provided the only means to check the charts in England for acts making the headlines. Interestingly I was never a fan of the Beatles or the Rolling Stones; my personal favourites at the time, apart from Elvis and Cliff Richard, were Billy J. Kramer and the Dakotas, Freddie and the Dreamers and the Rockin' Berries. In fact, I wrote to all three of them, as I had aspirations of becoming a pop star myself. One day I got this lovely letter from Freddie including his autograph. Years later, when I had arrived in Birmingham and was staying with my uncle Peter, he asked me if I had ever heard of the Rockin' Berries as the main singer only lived up the road from him. Unfortunately, by then the singer had moved out, although I believe I spoke to his mother. What a small world! I also loved the Bee Gees and their first hit 'Massachusetts'. Little did I know then that I would meet and interview the singer Robin Gibb in later years as a BBC broadcaster.

In my late teens a new phenomenon had hit the country, 'the showband scene'. This was a remarkable period in Irish life when the showbands epitomised glamour and generated mass hysteria among their followers. America had Elvis, England had the Beatles and we had the showbands. Newly created ballrooms were hurriedly constructed with breeze blocks and were in the shape of churches. Looking back now with rose tinted glasses, these bands and so-called ballrooms played an important role in the social life of rural Ireland at a time when there were very few alternative venues where young people could meet and enjoy themselves.

My own memories are of ballrooms like the Astoria in Bundoran and the Silver Slipper in Strandhill. Bundoran was nearest for me, and many a night was spent in long queues from about 10pm outside the ballrooms where the air smelt of Old Spice and Woodbine cigarettes. Pioneer pins (signifying abstinence from alcohol) were to be seen everywhere – evidence of straight living and good moral values. The Astoria would hold 2,000 people and the only available drink inside was a glass of milk or a Club orange.

Like Cliffoney Village Hall, the Astoria ballroom was a platform for what was a bizarre courting ritual: all the fellows would line up on one side of the dance floor and the woman on the other, each eyeing one another up – more in suspicion than in hope! Then the mad rush to find the prettiest girl to dance with. The greatest dread, the ultimate humiliation, was to cross the floor, only to lose the nerve at the last moment and do a George Best swerve towards the toilets, as if that had been your intention all along. Success brought the chance to meet the girl of your dreams and rejection brought you back to your mates with your tail between your legs and the old excuse, 'I didn't fancy her anyway'. It took a long time to build up the courage to cross the floor.

'Ballroom of Romance' in Glenfarne

The late arrivals, who had been filling up with drink at the local pubs, had no problems crossing the dance floor and put the rest of us to shame. At times like this, I wished I had the money to buy a couple of beers to give me some courage.

As a novice, I usually stayed with my friends. When we were down on our luck, the balcony was our sanctuary, where we could view the talent, or lack of it, and keep a check on who was making headway with whom. Refusals from girls came with a litany of excuses, such as 'ask me sister, she might fancy you' or 'I have a broken heel on me shoe'. The prettiest were always snapped up and, shall I say, the not so pretty ones stood patiently like wallflowers pretending not to care. Towards the end of the night the band would call for a lady's choice. This was the chance for a girl to ask you to dance. As you would expect, the good-looking chaps had the advantage. I seem to recall most of the girls wore their hair in a beehive style, with enough hair lacquer to sink a battle ship. They stood head and shoulders over many of us. Meanwhile the fellas had their hair smothered in Brylcreem, with enough grease to service a fleet of cars.

The Silver Slipper ballroom in Sligo was one venue that attracted huge crowds. The owner introduced the best musicians of the day from Ireland, England and America, including names that people had only heard of through Radio Luxembourg. Although I visited it many times, I couldn't afford the tickets for the likes of Roy Orbison and the Everly Brothers. In the seventies the venue also played host to U2, Eric Clapton and countless other top attractions.

So many generations met their other halves in the Silver Slipper. Perhaps the men were enticed in by the sign above the door which read 'Neath these portals tread some of the most beautiful girls in the world'. Hmmm, a slight exaggeration methinks!

Ireland at the time had one other hayshed constructed of galvanised roofing that was slightly different than the others. It stood at a crossroads in County Leitrim, some twenty-five miles away from my hometown. It was rather unsubtly called the 'Ballroom of Romance'. The owner of the ballroom, who was also the resident MC, introduced what he called 'the romantic interlude'. This short period of time, say twenty minutes, saw him and the band sing romantic songs. He would ask dancers to get together and get to know each other better. During this time the lights would be turned on and the menfolk encouraged to take their lady friends to the bar for a cup of tea or a mineral. Mind you, in my view the woman always looked better when the lights were dimmed! If you were fortunate enough to persuade a girl at a dance to accompany you outside for some 'fresh air' (invariably after buying her the obligatory Club orange), it was second heaven if you managed so much as a kiss. It is estimated that hundreds of happy marriages resulted from this interlude.

It's hard to believe now, but up until then matchmaking was a serious business in Ireland. When the parents of a young man thought it was time for him to take a wife they gave long and careful consideration to a suitable candidate. The match was then made, the parties sitting up all night, talking over terms, drinking whiskey and smoking tobacco. Those marriages were similar to the arranged marriages we see in Asian culture and were contracted in most instances without any regard to love, affection or any of the finer feelings. In some ways, matchmaking did work as it profiled people of the same age, similar background and education.

I remember falling in love – or what I thought was love – at the tender age of fifteen. I was at one of the many dances and fell for a girl from the other end of County Cavan, some fifty miles away from my home. At the time it might as well have been on another planet. She told me her surname was Brady. The next day I decided to look her up. To my amusement, I learned that almost everyone in Cavan was named Brady. Ah well, it was an age of innocence after all!

Around the same time, the 'marquee' craze hit rural Ireland. Basically, the entrepreneurs of the day erected a huge tent in the middle of a muddy field with not even basic facilities. As in so many aspects of life, I look back now with much joy and think, weren't those times wonderful? Heating didn't exist (despite the cold weather), paraffin oil was used to make the wooden dance floor slippery and ventilation was when the high winds blew half the tent away. It's worth pointing out, however, that, despite the primitive nature of the venues, the promoters of the dances made an absolute fortune.

The venues and facilities may have been basic, but who cared – we were young, full of life and enthusiasm, and with no cares for tomorrow. For me, ecstasy or cannabis did not come in tablet form; rather, it was a sweat-drenched night at a country crossroads, either under a giant canvas marquee or in the old hayshed.

PART-TIME WORK

I only had three part-time jobs in Ireland. The first was working behind the bar at Harrison's pub in Cliffoney. When I was about fifteen the owner, Michael Harrison, trusted me to run the place when he went on honeymoon with his wife Dympna. I clearly recall working behind the bar in November 1963, when the dreadful news reached us via radio that Irish American President John F. Kennedy had been shot and killed. A wave of grief that I had never witnessed before swept the village, and within a short space of time the pub was empty, the drinkers having gone home to take in this awful news. Kennedy had

Me working in Harrison's pub

recently visited Ireland and this made it all the more shocking for people.

Working in the bar provided me with so many memories; here was a rich vein of life I had never encountered before. Some customers came in for a 'quick one' whilst others came for longer sustenance. It was here that minor dramas were played out, heated arguments blew up, and over the counter deals were done. I loved my time working at Harrison's and could not understand why people drank that awful tasting Guinness. As for Paddy whiskey, it always amazed me, especially when they had the choice of Club orange or red lemonade. On the wall behind the counter was a large sign which read, 'Whatever you see or hear here, leave it here, then those not here, shall not hear'. I couldn't put it better myself – especially as during any quiet moment behind the bar I would be out front singing – taking off Buddy Holly or Elvis Presley, encouraged by the customers.

My second job saw me in Mullaghmore working as a gardener-cum-dogsbody for a retired lady doctor and her English-born husband who lived in a large bungalow on a hill facing the sea. The wages were poor and what pittance you got you certainly earned.

The man of the house spent most of his night time in conversation with captains of foreign ships around the world. He would very seldom surface during the day, or at least I didn't see him. The spacious back garden was a real eye opener, with hundreds of huge aerials rising like the morning dew into the sky. A large metal gate protected the house from intruders.

The lady was also a director of a well-known Sligo brewery. I would observe from an outside window many bottles of Club orange and red lemonade stacked high in the utility room but, despite being thirsty on a hot day with me tongue hanging out, I was never offered a mineral. Mind you, a plan was later hatched to get at the drink, which is not for wider circulation.

Most weekends were spent working on the gardens, where I would walk the three miles in and three miles home again. My tasks involved weeding the rose beds, but not pruning them as this was the job of a 'proper gardener'. To the front of the bungalow lay three beautiful manicured lawns, all at different levels. As anybody that has dealt with roses will tell you, trying to get between those that are grown in close proximity is no easy task, and my hands were cut to ribbons from the thorns. I once counted 400 roses. She also had hundreds of geraniums on her veranda, although I wasn't trusted to touch these. They did leave a lasting impression on me, however, and to this day I love to decorate my garden with these lovely flowers.

Another task was washing the lady's big Ford Zephyr motor car on the driveway. Such was the size of the car, and the diminutive size of the lady herself, I recall her having to prop herself up with four cushions to enable her to see out and drive. Despite my efforts, she picked holes in everything I did, and many a time she would whack me on the shoulders and shout 'straighten up young man and walk tall'. Even my sweeping out the garage wasn't to her standard.

In fairness, I learned a lot about gardening whilst working there, and still follow some of the lessons learnt to this very day, including always remove a weed if you see one, and never place a garden rake against a wall with its teeth facing out. Sally has nearly killed me on more than one occasion doing just that, when, on stepping on it, the rake handle would spring out and smack me in the gob.

Honesty was something the lady of the house was very strict on and she would often lay a few pence here and there around the yard, no doubt to test me out. I would always hand over any money to her, but not once did she thank me or give me any extra money in return for my honesty. The garage at their property was my sanctuary, when I would close the door and read the old newspapers stacked up on the shelves. A lot of them were English papers and that's when I first learned about the soccer teams, in particular Manchester United and Spurs.

During the summer of 1964, I landed a job at the Allingham Arms Hotel in Bundoran, now one of the largest in the north west of Ireland and home to Irish country music. I believe it came about on the recommendation of Michael Harrison, the village publican. At the time the hotel was no great shakes and accommodated around thirty people. My role was to look after the bar, milk two cows that were grazing in the fields behind the hotel, and be a general skivvy. My living quarters were on the outside, sharing a caravan-like hut with two others. Accommodation was pretty basic, with no toilets or running water. In addition to learning about work discipline, work relationships and the challenges of dealing with customers, I found myself working alongside men and woman of different ages, which suddenly gave me a different perspective on life.

During the day, my job was to order stock for the bar, and fill the shelves ready for the evening rush. First thing in the morning and early evening, I milked the cows in a corner of the field. In addition to there not being a shelter to prevent you from getting drenched in the rain, the biggest drawback was when the owner came with me. When he had consumed a few too many drinks he was a pain in the butt. He would insist on helping, but to be honest, he didn't know the cow's udder from her arse. Many times he keeled over or put his foot in the bucket!

I loved working behind the bar and enjoyed socializing with the guests. I benefited from the head barman leaving me alone to do my own thing, including drinking lots of red lemonade. Saturdays and Sundays were dancing and singing nights. The resident pianist and singer from Dublin was a man by the name of Crosby, and an uncle to John Stokes, by then part of the first boy band The Bachelors, who were huge in Ireland and the UK at the time.

Crosby was a brilliant entertainer and didn't dwell on his nephew's fame. Anyway, word got to him that I could sing a bit, so during the quiet days he would accompany me on the piano and I would belt out a few songs – practising for my moments of glory at the weekend. He did, however, insist on me learning some of The Bachelors' big hits. The weekends couldn't come quick enough, when he would call me up on stage. I would rather have belted out some of Elvis's songs as they were much easier to sing and more soothing on the listeners' ears, but nonetheless it was fantastic to have the chance to sing a few numbers in front of an audience. At the end of each song, people would ask for more and no better man than my good self to give them another one, two or, if they were very (un)lucky, three. I even got extra tips for my singing.

I was sad to leave at the end of August, when the management and Mr Crosby presented me with a small acoustic guitar. Just before leaving he advised me to buy a guitar tuition book called *Play a Tune a Day* by the world famous Bert Weedon. After weeks of trying, I managed to get it and began the practice outlined in the book. It was, however, full of complicated musical theory, so I struggled and only managed a few chords. The greatest problem I had was trying to tune the damn guitar.

What follows shows you what a small world we live in. Fast forward two decades, I'm now the sergeant in charge of Didcot Police Station when a new recruit, Geoff Weedon, is introduced to me. An unusual name, I thought, so I mentioned the famous Bert to him. I was shell shocked on hearing he was the oldest son of Bert. Months later the old man performed a charity gig at a nearby police station, when I had the pleasure of meeting him in person and telling him about his book and where he could shove it! A most delightful and engaging person, fabulous guitar player – one of the greatest in the world.

During that period I also got my first taste of performing at a radio station. Back then, of course, there wasn't the plethora of local or regional radio stations that there is today. RTE, the national broadcaster, was the only radio station in Ireland. I remember one summer's evening, during a break from the hotel, being interviewed in Bundoran on a radio programme that showcased emerging singing talent, no doubt on the word of Crosby. I had to sing a verse of a song called 'The Homes of Donegal'. I was nervous, messed up the lines and obviously didn't make a very good impression as I never heard from the station again. It pleased Nancy no end though, as she managed to listen in from Cloonkeen.

THE PANEL BEATER

At the end of 1964, following some wheeling and dealing by Nancy, I reluctantly agreed to take up a four-year apprenticeship as a panel beater at Maye's Motors in Sligo – a skilful job involving repairing and spraying damaged motor vehicles. To cut a long story short, without my knowledge, Nancy traded in my services when negotiating for a new Hillman Imp motor car. To add insult to injury, I was initially not allowed near the beautiful bright red car and it spent most of its time parked in front of the house until both Nancy and Michael got provisional driving licences. (Six months after this, the government, due to a backlog of people waiting to take their driving test, issued full licences to all provisional licence holders without any sort of test. What a joke. Talk about road safety!)

I recall it was at this time that the old style Ford Consul was fast disappearing and the country was becoming dotted with Volkswagens and Minis. Talking of Minis ... the skirts were getting increasingly shorter – to the horror of many a parent, but the delight of yours truly!

Maye's Motors was the main dealer for Opel, NSU and Hillman cars. It employed around twenty people: mechanics, salesman, store men and clerical staff. Privately owned by a local man who also owned a quarry, delivering concrete blocks and concrete, the garage had a large frontage, with petrol pumps and space to display new and used cars. Because of the quarry, delivery lorries were repaired in the yard, causing chaos and overcrowding when getting vehicles in and out.

As my first day approached, I was apprehensive – how was I going to get to Sligo, and what money was being offered? (Bizarrely this hadn't been discussed.) The day of reckoning arrived, when I took the bus into Sligo. I met the sales manager, Tom O'Brien, who doubled up as one of Ireland's national basketball coaches, and was shown to the panel beating workshop to be greeted by the boss. My boss, Pat

Front of Maye's Motors in Sligo when I started work there. (With Tom O'Brien, who took me on, and some brand new Opel motor cars)

Halley, a real gent from Kilkenny, was mad on hurling, which helped to break the ice.

The smell of paint spray was everywhere, entering my nose and mouth with its strong pungent odour. I noticed cars with damaged wings and bumpers were awaiting repair (at the time, car panels were not replaced with new ones like they are today). Red and black paint spray splashed over the workshop walls was a clear indication painting was par for the course. The workshop was separate from the main body of the garage. Having put on the deep blue overalls, which were too big around the arse (the story of my life), I was sent to the office to be told the 'do's and don'ts'. In summary: there was to be no borrowing the mechanics tools without permission – not a problem, as I wouldn't know how to use them anyway. The most important news, my weekly wages, came as a shock: one pound and ten shillings a week, with no overtime. What? I was getting more doing seasonable work at the Allingham Arms, I thought to myself. That said, it was a job, which was better than nothing.

The first week went quickly, getting to know the apprentice mechanics, who were nearly all from Sligo, with 'townie' accents you could cut with a knife; streetwise and well versed in the ways of life.

The owner would divide his time between the quarry and the garage, which was just as well for us. He was a lovely man but prone to outbursts, mainly directed towards the lorry drivers, whom he blamed for everything under the sun (probably blaming them for losing money whilst the lorries were being repaired). In his rage, he would dance a jig in the yard, and everyone stayed well clear until he disappeared.

One day, I was talking football with one of the mechanics inside when the owner appeared in the yard in his usual boisterous mood, jumping up and down and shouting. As he finished, I put my hands outside the door and gave him a round of applause. In he comes demanding to know who did the clapping (young Wymbs by now was long gone under a car). Thankfully, nothing was said, but I was banished indefinitely from entering their workshop.

The job itself was more skilful than I imagined and I had to knuckle down and learn the ropes. Getting to work from home was also proving difficult as I didn't have sufficient money to pay the fare. Most of the time I resorted to thumbing lifts. You had to be very lucky, as the few cars passing were already full, and, as a consequence, I was often late for work.

Thankfully, spraying the repaired vehicles, which were mostly red or black, only happened once a week. There were few health and safety guidelines at the time, and despite the need to wear a mask to prevent inhaling the fumes we often ignored this advice.

There were occasions when, for days after spraying, I would be spitting up paint particles. Goodness knows, I'm lucky to be still alive.

At lunchtime, I would wander off into the main workshop and watch the mechanics sanding down asbestos linings for use in brake pads. Dust and fibres everywhere, including on my cheese sandwiches. Almost all of those men died relatively young, and it is my belief that in most cases doctors in Ireland issued death certificates without a post mortem being carried out to determine the exact cause of death. I believe this was medical practice at the time.

As we now know, asbestos is a severe health risk when the fibres are airborne, and it kills around 5,000 workers a year in Britain. Later in life, during my days working with the coroner in Oxford, I was particularly interested in asbestos related diseases and its effects on the lining of the lungs. I learnt that it can take up to fifty years for the negative effects of asbestos to develop and then there's no cure. I often think of my friends in the garage who are no longer with us, and of course my own mortality and the abundance of fibres on my cheese sandwiches. Funnily enough, I am still partial to the odd cheese sandwich; can't beat them with a little pickle.

NORTH TO ALASKA, HENRY?

As each month passed, my confidence in the job grew. I was now able to dismantle wings and bonnets before repairing them with filler and spraying them. What's more, my welding improved and the boss was relatively happy. But was I? No.

One of the problems was I got bored easily and would end up heading for town, a couple of hundred yards away, to read the papers in the newsagents'. With no money to buy them, I was run out of the shops many times and warned not to come back. Being a glutton for punishment, I'd be in again the following day, and would read the papers behind a stack of shelves.

Meanwhile, back at the ranch, or should I say garage, there was no trace of Henry. 'Where's he gone now?' was the cry from the boss. Every lame excuse under the sun was used to keep me out of trouble. By now, I was into my second year, and instead of borrowing tools, I became the proud owner of my own tool kit. It was a strange decision to buy them as by this time I had finally come to the conclusion that manual work was not for me and a change of direction to some less arduous work would be in the best interests of all concerned.

Thoughts crossed my mind: what about the prior 'calling' to the priesthood? This might be better than being under a car on a wet day. It did make me think, but by this time my language had become rather 'agricultural', and I guessed the clergy wouldn't touch me with a barge pole, and rightly so.

As time went on, I realised I wasn't really pulling my weight, and I was spending more time discussing football, music and dancing. They all came before panel beating. The one good thing about the job was that it gave me the opportunely to learn to drive and eventually pass my test. Meanwhile, Michael and Nancy were still doing their utmost to keep the roads of Ireland free from traffic with their erratic driving. That reminds me, on one occasion the local postman, John Higgins, a man in his sixties (who only ever rode a postman's bike), purchased an old banger. He wasn't sure how to use the brake and clutch, and in his endeavour to go around a corner on a country lane, landed me and him upside down in a ditch three foot deep in water. That was the end of his driving and nearly the end of me as well.

Late nights and early mornings did not suit me one iota. Monday mornings were real killers and, after I inadvertently ran over her pet poodle (sorry!), Nancy put her foot down and stopped me using the car. Getting back from Bundoran at five o'clock in the morning and up again for eight was not the best preparation for a heavy day's work. As a group, we would walk the eight or nine miles' home. Nancy, like all mothers, would not sleep properly until I had got home. She was the devil for laying traps to check the time I got in, often placing a couple of pots and pans in the bedroom doorway, making sure I'd trip over them and, in so doing, wake up the whole house.

It seemed that no sooner was I in bed than Michael began banging on the door. I'd have a drop of tea, and then began the long chase down the road to catch the bus. On occasions the bus driver would feel sorry for me and, should my head appear above the brow of the hill half a mile away, he would wait, much to the annoyance of some of the passengers. I'd hop on, and there would be a round of applause from the bus driver, conductor and some of the passengers, but long faces on others who didn't see the funny side of delaying the bus and keeping them waiting.

The bus conductor, who was prone to whistling well-known songs of the time, would shout out, 'give us a verse of "North to Alaska", Henry'. The song was a means of getting a free bus ride to work. There can be few things worse than me belting out a song at eight in the morning. Some people put their hands to their ears, whilst others clapped and wanted more. By the time the bus arrived in Sligo, I was hoarse from all the singing, but little did I care as it meant a free ride for me. The songs, however, had to change, as the passengers travelling on the bus had heard them all before. I firmly believe that some of them would have paid my fare just to shut me up.

On the way home from work on the Monday evening I would drop into Terence Leonard's home and listen to the Top Ten Chart of Irish showband songs. Mrs Leonard, God be good to her, always made sure it was switched on for me and fed me as well.

In my third year of work I'd had no pay increase, and only fifty 'Players' cigarettes at Christmas, which I sold on as I didn't smoke. I was fed up and hated my work, and a lot of my time was spent laying under a car nodding off and doing nothing. It was a dreadful existence and my only salvation came at six in the evening when work finished. I did, however, become good friends with all the staff, including Eugene Deering, Sean McGloin and Frank McSharry who were like brothers to me and, in my absence, covered up for me many a time by telling the boss I was taking a car out for a test run. Beyond forging these friendships, and helping out at the petrol station in the evenings to earn a few extra bob, the only other perk was that I could make use of an old battered Mini Van on a Friday night. The boss was never that keen on me taking it out, but at nine in the evening with nobody around, it was mine for the weekend.

Mind you, it had to be back before staff arrived on Monday morning, otherwise I was for the high jump. I made great use of the van, especially in the evenings, when eight of us would cram into it and head for a dance fifty miles away, five in the back and three in the front. I never had any money, so the lads would pay for me to get in.

For some reason a person with a car had many friends back then! So many mates enriched my earlier life in Ireland, including Seamus Moore, Poric Gallagher, Paddy Gallagher, Terence Leonard, Danny Warnock, John Barry, John and Joe Watters, Joseph, Gus and Liam

Old mates of mine, Terry Rooney and Terence Leonard

McHugh, Patsy Fowley, Donal Conway, Seamus Conway, Mark Hannon, Tommy Kenny, Mick McGowan, Willie Gilmartin, Terry Rooney, John Brennan and Hugh Quinn. Thanks also to all the others, too many to mention (you know who you are).

Into the dancehall at last and the same well-worn old routine: men on one side and girls on the other. The good-looking girls were all dancing and the 'wallflowers' standing like statues waiting to be asked to dance. I noticed this girl – probably the best looking of the 'wallflowers' – staring towards me out of the corner of one eye. I thought my luck was in and made my way to ask her to dance. Just then, out of nowhere, came another chap from the other direction, who got there first. If I didn't have bad luck, I'd have no luck at all. It was only later on that I noticed the poor girl was cross-eyed!

Come the end of the evening and the same motley crew would pile in the back of the van singing Elvis songs, which made the journey go that much faster. With such a shortage of transport, it was not uncommon to travel in the back of a manure laden cattle lorry – no wonder girls gave us the cold shoulder! To make matters worse, there were no showers or baths in those days and, despite a dash of Old Spice (usually over the shirt), the smell must have been something else! Oh happy days!

A NEW DREAM

Whilst working at the garage I became particularly friendly with Maurice Gilmartin, who was slightly older than me and had just finished college. Whilst awaiting his exam results to join the banking profession, Maurice had taken on a part-time job in the office. I knew him from football where we played against each other. Anyway, each Monday morning the English *News of the World* newspaper appeared from somewhere and was the source of debate among us teenagers. Ireland at this time was very much under the thumb of the Catholic church and papers like this, carrying pictures of girls and saucy stories, were not welcome.

Thumbing through this paper in the summer of '67 proved to be a turning point in my life. We found a recruitment campaign for police officers in England, and joked about us riding police bikes and driving high-powered police cars. Nothing more was said, until a week or so later I received an official looking letter addressed to me with English postage.

I'd never been to England and was somewhat concerned. I opened it and enclosed was this glossy brochure, together with an application form to apply for the police. I hadn't requested it; my mate obviously had. When I had read all the details I thought, 'could this be my way out of the garage?' Now, what was I to do? With little education, poor eyesight and facing a minimum height requirement, I didn't think I stood a chance. However, with gentle persuasion from Maurice over a cup of tea in the office and nothing to lose, we filled in the application form.

The brochure gave a list of the thirty police forces recruiting at that time; the only problem being, I was only just about tall enough for ten of them. Maurice[3] was now more enthusiastic than me and cut the ten out, rolled them up into a ball and placed them in a cup. It was like a raffle! Out came Oxford City. I had only ever heard of Oxford University, and was not even sure where in England it was. With nothing to lose, I posted the application form and forgot all about it. I heard nothing for the best part of a month, but then one morning a letter arrived outlining the enquires to be made into my background and other details.

By now I'd lost all interest in the garage and couldn't wait to leave. I did not believe for a second I had any chance of getting into the Oxford Police, but I was willing to give it a go. On finding out my intentions, the local sergeant in Cliffoney, a cautious man at the best of times, asked me to pop in and see him at the station. He was very

---

[3] Maurice's career path also took him to England in the same year, see Chapter 9.

helpful, but warned me not to raise my hopes too high as the police in England were quite strict in their recruitment. After a round of questions, he measured me and I was just under five foot nine, which was a bit of a concern. Anyway he said not to worry and off I went.

Another month went by, and at last I received a letter informing me to sit the entrance examination in the Sligo Garda station in October of that year. Time to panic: I was never any good at exams. I took the bull by the horns and visited a local retired school teacher, a lovely lady by the name of Bridie Jennings, who lived near the church. At the time I read quite a lot – mainly newspapers and a neighbour's *Reader's Digest* magazine – but passing the exams would not be easy. For the next two months, Miss Jennings prepared me for the exams through a series of two-hour sessions (three times a week) plus homework. It was tough, but the end result might be a job in the police force, so it would be worth it. I worked really hard on a range of different subjects and come the day of the exam, I felt quietly confident.

Now the hour had arrived when all my learnings would be put to the test. I was met at the Garda station in Sligo by a sergeant, who took me upstairs into a dingy room full of cigarette smoke. Five minutes later an inspector came in with a sealed envelope containing the exam papers, which he handed to me. The sergeant sat down by the turf fire. There were five exam sheets, English, maths, general knowledge, history and geography, with half an hour allowed for each subject. The sergeant took a look at the papers, shook his head and wandered off. 'Take your time son, no rush,' he said. 'I'll be back after lunch.' If only mobiles phones were around then, or that television show with '*phone a friend*'.

I managed to get through all five papers, and true to his word the sergeant came back about four hours later, which gave me the opportunity to double check everything. I struggled a bit with the maths, but felt happy enough with the other subjects. The sergeant perused my papers and told me frankly that I should be applying for the Garda Síochána (Irish police) instead of going to England. I did consider this, but my Irish by then was very poor and I didn't think I was tall enough to join the Garda.

There was then the awful waiting, not knowing whether or not I had passed. At last, the letter arrived. I quickly tore it open and held my breathe ... I had passed! I was told to present myself for an interview and medical examination in Oxford in January 1968. Success! I was elated, it was the best Christmas I had ever had.

One concern I did have, however, was the eyesight test. As a child I had worn glasses for about a week and then smashed them up due to being teased about them at school. I hadn't had my eyes tested since and realised from reading that I was a bit near sighted, so it was off to see the village lady doctor to explain my dilemma. She agreed it might be a problem as the police were quite strict on this. 'I'll get hold of a chart by tomorrow, and check how many lines you can read' was her passing remark. The following day, I could only manage to see half way down the chart. She shook her head and whispered, 'you will struggle'. She then handed me the dreaded chart and told me to learn it off parrot fashion in preparation for the test in England. For the next month I read it so much that I knew it backwards.

Maye's Motors dinner dance, (far right in back row), a week before I left for England

Following receipt of the interview letter I somewhat prematurely told my friends I was moving on and gave in my notice at work. I still had another year left of my apprenticeship and it didn't dawn on me at the time that this was just the first stage of the process, I hadn't actually got the job yet! On top of that, how would I pay to get over to England? In those days flights were rare and expensive, and the boat journey was long and arduous.

The end of January couldn't come quickly enough. With the help of my friends and family I gathered enough money to pay the train and plane fare. I had never been in the sky before and to say I was frightened would be an understatement.

With a heavy heart, Nancy accompanied me to Sligo railway station. She waited with tears in her eyes as I boarded the train to set off on a journey into the unknown. On a cold January afternoon in 1968, at the age of twenty, with my meagre possessions and £6 in my pocket, I boarded the Aer Lingus plane at Dublin Airport bound for Birmingham … excited but very apprehensive about what lay ahead.

Chapter Five

BOBBY ON THE BEAT

LEAP INTO THE UNKNOWN

Near to our arrival in England, I was transfixed by the lights over Birmingham. I prayed like I never did before that we would land safely. Thankfully we did and I managed to find my way out, following everyone else who seemed to know what they were doing and where they were going.

Outside the airport were lights, noises and crowds of people. What was I doing? I asked myself. And to compound the problem, I couldn't see my uncle Peter. Would he recognise me? (Uncle Peter was Nancy's younger brother who had emigrated to Birmingham in the late fifties. I think I had only met him once when he came back to Ireland in the early sixties.)

All sorts of negative thoughts crossed my mind. Everything seemed strange: the people spoke with a funny accent and they didn't seem to see each other. They all buzzed around like bees.

Then out of nowhere, and much to my relief, I heard a voice shout 'Henry'. It was my uncle Peter. We talked a lot about the police in the car journey to his house, which was about ten miles away. I was still apprehensive about what lay ahead. This was only the first part of the journey. I stayed overnight with uncle Peter and his wife Barbara and then took a bus to Oxford the next day. (In later years Sally and I saw quite a bit of them and their family.)

On arrival at the bus station in Oxford at about eight at night, I

Oxford Police Station when I arrived in 1968

was lost and bewildered in a strange city with no family or friends. I managed to pull myself together and found a person who looked official to guide me to the police station. In the distance Oxford police station stood out like a beacon in the night, a huge building with lights everywhere. At last a place to rest my head for a while.

I went to the front counter and spoke to a police officer at the desk. I told him who I was and that I wished to see the Chief Constable. The look on his face said it all. 'I don't think the Chief will want to see you at this time of the night, but come upstairs, we were expecting you.' At this moment the initiation of my ambition began. I met some off-duty police officers who really looked after me, and some have remained friends for life. I was given my own room, a real luxury, and shown the bathrooms, sitting room and canteen. I slept well that night.

The following day, a sergeant took me for the formal interview with the Chief Constable. On entering this huge office with a large oval table in the middle, I was struck by the sight of a bar to the side, with optics hanging down. Then the large open fire made me feel at home. The Chief was an older man and sat on his own at the head of the table. He shook my hand and welcomed me to Oxford. The interview lasted half an hour.

With the passage of time I have no idea what questions were asked. I left the room and was told to wait outside for a decision to be made. The same sergeant took me back in again and the Chief stood up, shook my hand and said 'I like you. You have a nice way about you. Not the brightest we have ever had but, subject to a medical examination later today, you will be the last Oxford City Police officer to join before the big amalgamation in a couple of months' time.' I was over the moon, but nervous about the medical examination. As for the word 'amalgamation', I didn't have a clue what it meant.

Later that day I attended the police surgeon's office in the centre of Oxford, with the same sergeant looking after me. He made me aware that the doctor was a friendly older man from Northern Ireland who I would get on well with. As predicted, the doctor made me welcome and enquired about my health. I then undertook a strict medical. I was asked to stand against the wall for my height measurement. Knowing that I was not blessed in the height department, I was cute enough to put some sticky plasters on my heels under two pairs of socks to give me some extra height. In addition, when the piece of wood rested on the top of my head, the doctor didn't think to look down to my feet, which gave me the chance to stand on my toes. I was almost 5 foot 10 inches! I was chuffed when given the news as 5 foot 9 inches was the minimum height at the time for acceptance into the police.

Next for the eyesight test, and what about the lines I learned from the good doctor's chart in Ireland? What if they were different in England? Fortunately, I passed with flying colours. The final piece of the jigsaw was a colour-blindness chart. This was news to me as I had never even heard of the term before. The doctor emphasised the importance of this test and that I had to pass it. To be honest I didn't have a clue what all the fuss was about. Again, no problems. I was now fit to be sworn in as a police officer.

Oxford City Police beckoned and I joined on 2nd February 1968 as recruit number 83. The force was now up to strength, with 250 officers. It was time for the new uniform and helmet, which still made me look small in comparison to other officers.

The standard issue of uniform back then was one lightweight tunic, two pairs of trousers for the summer, and the same for the winter in heavy weight. You were also issued with five blue shirts, two black ties, a heavy and a lightweight overcoat, which reached the pavement as you walked, a black cape for over your shoulders, one helmet, one cap and two pairs of gloves (one black leather and one white cotton for traffic duties), handcuffs, a wooden truncheon, and finally a whistle. You were also given a boot or shoe allowance, which was claimed each year. The shirts at the time did not have collars, and a stud was used to fasten them. Collars had to be starched, which cut the neck off you. You would always identify a policeman when in civilian clothes by the red stud mark and red ring around their necks. You could wear the shirts for months, especially in the winter time, as all that needed to be visible was the collar. The trousers had a special pocket for the truncheon which ran down the outside of your leg and was most uncomfortable, not to mention at times embarrassing when you sat down.

Next stop, training college. At the ripe old age of twenty I was going back into the classroom, except this time I was excited about it and would learn all things thrown at me. It opened up an entirely new world and I wasn't going to mess it up.

TRAINING COLLEGE

The police training college, Eynsham Hall, a stately mansion standing proud amid 3,000 acres of rolling parkland, was based in Oxfordshire and close to my lodgings at the police station. I was fortunate at the time as, unlike me, recruits from other forces hundreds of miles away had long journeys to travel. Again, Lady Luck played her part, with the next batch of recruits commencing training later that month.

The training college was a cold, dreary place which was run along military lines. All recruits were billeted either in the college or in outside huts. I shared a large dormitory inside with three others. You

A road traffic accident exercise at the Police Training College,
Eynsham Hall, 1967 (a few months before I arrived there)

had a set routine each morning, including the bed having to be made
in a military way. Although all new to me, I was lucky as the fella
next to me was a military man and he taught me how to press my
uniform and polish my boots for the morning parade. Creases were
sharpened with a hot iron on brown paper, boots polished to a mirror
finish and then protected under the bed for the night. In the morning
every speck of dust had to be removed from the uniform and helmet.
The drill parade was followed by a hearty breakfast.

The training was a real eye opener. Other recruits came from many
backgrounds and disciplines: teaching, accountancy, journalism, civil
servants, military men and police cadets. Some of the cadets were
the bane of other recruits' lives. They were basically police apprentices,
joining up on leaving school at seventeen, who had no powers, but
after two years shadowing police officers and legal training, they were
streets ahead of us beginners. Some of them were arrogant, big headed
and know-alls. The phrase 'if you had an elephant, they'd have a box
to put it in' springs to mind.

There were two classes, each consisting of twenty recruits in the
juniors, roughly the same in the intermediate, and the same again in
the seniors. Overall, over 120 recruits would be there at any one time.

With my room mates at Eynsham Hall (good friends at the time, but we all went our separate ways)

It was a steep learning curve for me, which meant I studied at every opportunity to try and keep up with the rest of the recruits during exam times. It was not easy as the training was very concentrated and highly competitive, with weekly tests and exams which had to be passed or you were out. It was a tough time, with the pain of the stamina runs, the drunk and disorderly practicals, and the harsh swimming lessons just adding to the turmoil. Life in the college was tough, although there were some rare acts of kindness and enlightenment from certain members of staff.

The obligatory haircut every fortnight was a harrowing experience. The local butcher, armed with clippers the size of garden shears, tore into your head like a reaper mowing oats. There was never any need for Brylcreem, just some antiseptic cream to heal the wounds. After clipping the heads of a class of twenty, there was enough hair to fill a pillowcase.

Classes began at nine in the morning and finished at five. Some weekends you were free to travel home, though I tended to stay and study. On many occasions I made a pig's ear of practical road traffic accidents, or worse still killed the dummy in first aid by extracting instead of blowing air into its mouth. One weekend in four was duty weekend, when I patrolled the grounds and made pocket notes of anything unusual. This was to prepare you for the life of a police officer once you passed out from training. You had to be on your toes as traps were set: a supposedly courting couple rustling in the bushes, or a light going on and off along the terrace. This was to test your powers of observation and how you dealt with things. Big trouble ensued in the morning if you missed them or failed to fully investigate; you'd be up in front of the deputy commandant and would get a rollicking, with punishment points to add to your woes.

One of the hardest duties at the college was the morning parades, when you were on the square at half seven each day. The drill sergeant was a hard man, complete with a slashed peak on his cap. He took a disliking to me from the word go, and I'm convinced that if it hadn't been for my own class instructor he would have got rid of me. He was a typical loudmouth, ranting and raving, using expletives at every opportunity; mind you, I was handy at them myself, but you daren't answer back. It didn't help that I had two left feet on the drill square, which drove him nuts. As I did not have military training, I found this exercise very difficult. I became a liability to the other officers as you had to keep in step during the marching parade. I didn't, and those behind me experienced difficulties, tripping over me. The drill exercise was a way of imposing a steely timetable and a cold discipline with excessively tight rules of dress and behaviour and a harshness to either make or break you.

The sergeant in charge of physical education was cut from the same cloth as the drill instructor: big, arrogant and full of himself. Mind you, he did have good reason to be sure of himself as he had represented Britain at the Rome Olympics in 1960 for swimming. I've never seen any person who could swim like him. I just couldn't believe my eyes when he did four full lengths under water. My first brush with the pool came when he pushed me in the deep end and left me struggling for ages until I was rescued. I thought I was going to drown. In all fairness to the sergeant, by the time he had finished with me I was able to swim a couple of lengths of the pool.

There was great emphasis on physical fitness and self-defence, particularly on how to deal with someone threatening to use a knife. I gained in confidence as the final few weeks drew near. You learned how to give evidence in dummy courts, make and take statements, and learn the law definitions off parrot fashion. The teaching was a mixture of theory (learning the law) and practical exercises in making arrests. By this time the drill sergeant had become a bit more civilised to me. During the final drill session, he placed me at the rear, no doubt not wanting to show himself up at the big passing-out parade with all the families and dignitaries present.

In the final week of the three month course, there was a farewell dinner and dance, when the local girls were bused in to join us. I don't remember a lot about it now. The college had its own bar, and despite the hardship, I never touched the liquor until the final dinner, when red and white wine were available. I took a swig from the glass of the red stuff but it tasted like vinegar.

Then came the big day itself, when we were informed we had passed all the exams and were now probationary police officers. I did okay and came tenth in the final examination out of my class of twenty. My

My police training class before the passing-out parade in May 1968
(3rd from right, middle row)

sergeant instructor was brilliant, even giving me private tuition in the evenings. (I later found out that he sadly lost his life in a swimming accident some years later.)

Two from my class of twenty failed and were rejected by their respective forces. The final passing-out parade is now just a faint memory, but I remember that all the recruits had families there to see them except me. It's funny, I didn't think a lot about it at the time because of the excitement. When I passed out, it was such a relief. The three months had left their mark. The constant studying, discipline, loss of freedom, and institutional lifestyle were aspects of life I had not encountered before. If it were not for the fear of failure, I would have given up. My experience was not unique, however, as others felt the same. I must say it made me a better person – a more caring creature, and one better equipped for the hard knocks in life. Like everybody else who had been through such an intense period of training, we could not wait for the real job to start.

OXFORD CITY NEW RECRUIT

Oxford is known as the City of Dreaming Spires, a historic city that has an international reputation both in its own right and for its universities. About three million tourists visit the city every year to see its beautiful buildings. For hundreds of years it had been home to scholars and royalty and its place in history is assured.

When returning from training college as a newcomer I had a lot to learn about this famous city. Like plenty of people at the time, I believed Oxford had just one university. I was wrong, and had to quickly learn the names and locations of the 40 or so colleges dotted all around a radius of a couple of miles of the city centre.

What Oxford did have at the start of 1968 was one police force, although this was soon to change. Oxford City Police was nearing its centenary year, having been formed in 1869; however, like my own life at the time, big changes were afoot. On returning from college to my home station, Oxford City Police Force had changed and was now part of a wider Thames Valley Police, which incorporated Berkshire, Buckinghamshire and Oxfordshire. This change made sense to me as all these areas had lots of chiefs but not enough lower ranks on the ground. The expertise and resources could now be shared by all.

Other recent changes to Oxford's police force at the time included becoming the first force in the country to have its own drug squad, as well as a dedicated cycle team of two officers. For me it was an incredible sight seeing the hundreds of bikes lined up against the college walls.

My return from college was greeted with a visit to the new chief superintendent, a likeable man whom I had not met before. He read out passages from my training college report. It was excellent and better than I ever expected. 'Don't worry about the two left feet,' he said. 'You don't need to march on the beat.' He shook my hand and wished me luck. I was then assigned to my tutor constable, a giant man of six foot four inches, for the next six weeks. He was brilliant and, mindful that I was one of the smaller officers and not wanting to make me look silly, would walk in the road when he could and let me walk on the footpath; thus allowing me some much needed height advantage. I learned a lot from him, some of which was even police work. His parting words to me were 'never try and nick them when the sods outnumber you'.

After the six weeks' training, I was now let loose on my own, armed with all the knowledge drummed into me at training college, to uphold the law and serve the public in every way unsupervised. Despite this, I remained on probationary period for two years, with law and practical classes once a week. Again you had to pass them, otherwise you were out. I was attached to all the different departments for a couple of weeks at a time: criminal investigation department (CID), drug squad, traffic department, fraud squad, admin office and the coroner's department – which I found the most interesting. All heads of departments had to report back on your attitude, knowledge of the law and a most likely career move in the future. It was later obvious from my reports that I was destined to join the CID and become a detective.

I was full of apprehension and felt like a nervous wreck. I had to expect the unexpected at all times. There can be few occupations where the demands are more varied because of the range and complexity of police work, which was a major challenge to me.

It is worth remembering that the late '60s was a time when the popular image of a police officer was the local 'bobby' patrolling his beat, chatting to children and adults, perhaps giving some timely advice to teenagers who might be in danger of going astray, or assisting families and communities at times of trauma. Much of the image was due, in some respects, to television programmes of the time, like *Dixon of Dock Green* and *Z Cars*. The reality of police work, however, meant dealing with offenders for thefts, assaults and public order offences, as well as attending traffic accidents and sudden deaths. This opened up a whole new way of life that, previously, I was only aware of through reading the newspapers and watching television. My first arrest was a beggar who was drunk and disorderly. He struggled violently until we got him handcuffed and put him in the cells.

Away from work, yet not quite away from the police station, I was living on the second floor of the station. Life was good. I had my own room, with a bed big enough for a giant, basically taking up all the space. I could have opened the door, closed the window and prepared the breakfast all without getting out of bed. There was a huge bath, showers, kitchen, washing machine, tumble dryer and laundry room, and the bed was made for you every morning. In addition, there was a gym, a big ballroom/club room, snooker table, staff canteen and luxury bar. What more could any man want?

The dos and don'ts were numerous, including the time you had to get up in the morning to allow the cleaners in, and the time you had to be in when not on duty. There were, however, many ways to get around those rules, like making sure the night duty sergeant was on tea break if you arrived late. Normally the duty constable would see or hear nothing and ignored you. Where necessary, the open ground floor window was another entry route.

My bedroom was situated directly above the cells and prisoners' exercise yard and, although two floors up, I would hear them shouting whilst I was trying to sleep in the day (when on night duty). To make matters worse, the kennels for lost and found dogs were also in the backyard and so there was a constant noise of dogs barking. That said, I was lucky because some of the lads had their rooms to the front of the station and were constantly awakened during the night by shouting from released prisoners. On more than one occasion I recall that buckets of water were thrown from the third floor onto the departing prisoners below. In the morning all hell would break loose and a big investigation would begin to find out who the culprit was. Naturally, nobody would own up to this terrible deed.

One of my real joys at that time was having a hot bath. I'd never had a real bath in my life and it was a novelty; only problem, I nearly drowned in them. Police officers in the main are big men, and the size of the baths would fit two chaps like me. Such was my love for the bath, I got into trouble on more than one occasion for overstaying my welcome. You see, while the door was locked and others were knocking on it to get me out, I would spend a couple of hours topping up the lovely hot water once it cooled down and then splashing around like a hippo in a swimming pool. Anyway, after a while I got my marching orders and was only allowed to stay in it for twenty minutes at a time. In addition, I was banned from using it after midnight because of the noise coming from the water tank.

It was also the first time I experienced a large communal shower and was somewhat embarrassed when others joined me. I got a real shock one day when a policewoman popped her head around the corner waiting for her turn to get in. She had a long look, nodded her head, smiled and left me wondering what she was looking at!

Another first for me was seeing a man with multiple pairs of shoes in his room. I didn't think men had more than one pair. The laundry room was a real treat as well as it was full of lovely coloured, washed

Off duty, at St Giles' Fair

and ironed shirts, jumpers, and trousers. I had a choice of what to wear and, not thinking this one through, was convinced that no one would be any the wiser if I borrowed them. On one occasion I borrowed a shirt for a dance and, when I tried it on, it was more like an overcoat, going all the way down to my toes. Oh well, I had nothing else to wear, so it would have to do. Unfortunately I found out in no uncertain terms that it belonged to a big Scotsman who needed it the same night; he nearly killed me when he found out.

Life in a city was very different to village life in Ireland. Suddenly I was introduced to new foods. It was a real delight for me to visit the local Chinese restaurant in Queen Street, in the centre of Oxford. I had sampled some of Nancy's homemade curries at home, but never with rice. I thought rice was only used in puddings. I soon savoured their delicious meals, on some rest days visiting the restaurant a couple of times a day. On other occasions I would join my mates in some pub at lunchtime and be given an enormous loaf of crusty bread, a lump of cheese and a spoonful of pickle, all to be washed down with a pint of 'best' bitter. It was my introduction to a traditional English lunchtime concoction called 'a ploughman's lunch', which I had never heard of and was definitely not to my liking. It was at those times that I longed for mother's traditional meals of boiled bacon and cabbage!

On the subject of home, I was still homesick. I missed my family, the mountains, the sea and the smell of turf fires. Unfortunately I was unable to ring home at the time because my parents didn't have a phone. I did, though, speak to Nancy a few times from a telephone kiosk in Oxford to a newly installed one in Cliffoney. It was, however, a long-drawn-out process. In fact, by the time the switch board operator connected you, the sun had set and was about to rise again. Bless her, mother also wrote to me once a week and sent me the local rag, the *Sligo Champion*, to keep me abreast of what was going on back home.

In the three months since I had left Ireland my wages had risen from one pound, ten shillings a week in Sligo to twelve pounds a week, and on top of that I benefited from free lodgings and lots of perks. Single men's quarters as it was called would require another book to do justice to my twelve months there. The quarters had fifteen officers there at any one time. We had great fun and, with most of the other men being older than me, they took me under their wing. As you can imagine, there was plenty of leg pulling, mickey taking and tricks played on one another. I was on the receiving end on more than one occasion. Without divulging names, I would like to share one such incident which in hindsight served me right.

It was Saturday afternoon, and I was obviously misbehaving in the sitting room, up to my old tricks winding my colleagues up, whilst they were watching cricket. Cricket, to me, was as boring as watching paint dry. Once the match was over, I had nodded off and was easy prey. Three of them, all rugby players, grabbed me, stripped me down to my underpants and handcuffed me to the metal radiator by the front window, which they opened wide to freeze me bits off. Lights switched off, and gone. Being a Saturday there was nobody around to hear me shout for help. Three hours later and now in an awful state, bursting to use the toilet, a canteen cleaner popped her head around the corner and raised the alarm. A short while later all three colleagues appeared rather the worst for drink, and unlocked me. The young trainee was a quiet boy for a long time after that incident. The main culprit, a lovely chap, has sadly passed on to his heavenly beat in the sky.

BOBBY ON A BIKE

Having gone from working as a panel beater in Sligo just months earlier, it was now such a great feeling to be training as a police officer, patrolling the beat with a few more pennies in the pocket and, more importantly to me, having my own police vehicle … my bike! I have clear memories of cycling at regulation pace (slow) up the Banbury Road in Oxford on a balmy summer's evening and feeling cool and confident in my full police uniform and helmet, despite having to cycle slowly as when riding the oversized bike – like the baths they were built for big men – with a large truncheon dangling in my trousers pocket, tears came to my eyes. I was only just able to reach the ground with my feet, and would also spend time battling to keep my helmet on in high winds. At this time the police had a garage at the rear of the station where a dedicated team of mechanics would mend the police cars and cycles. I felt more at home there and would visit them regularly and tell them of my exploits in Maye's Motors in Sligo.

On my beloved police bike

I recall one time, as I cycled along, I was temporarily distracted by two ladies in miniskirts walking on the footpath towards me (this was the 'swinging sixties', remember) and with my eyes turning towards them I ended up cycling into the back of a parked black Morris Minor, landing head first on the road. In the process, I ripped my police trousers and badly grazed my knees. Serves me right, you might say! Of course, as is often the way when accidents occur in public, I played down the incident to concerned passers-by and quickly jumped to my feet and dusted off my crooked helmet. To be honest, my beloved police bike was far more traumatised by the accident than I was. The girls quickly came to my rescue to check that I was okay. When jumping back on the saddle I had to negotiate riding a bike with two square shaped wheels that made clunking sounds on every turn (it would have benefited hugely from the mechanical skills of my uncle Pat back in Cliffoney). What a fool, I thought afterwards. Why didn't I stay down and pretend I was unconscious, then the girls may have given me mouth to mouth resuscitation? Taught me a good lesson though ... always keep your eyes on the road!

The city centre beat was my favourite. It came to life at about half seven in the morning, when all the office workers (mainly girls) would pass by. I stood there and tried not to make it obvious I was looking at them. We came back into the station for breakfast at eight or nine for 45 minutes. Then back on the street, this time viewing the shop window dressers. At that hour of the morning I wasn't quite sure if the girls were real or mannequins. Morning rush hour traffic would sometimes be of concern when you had to issue penalty tickets or do traffic duty, but most of the time was spent directing visitors to different colleges, arresting shoplifters or posing for photographs with tourists. The latter was an occupational hazard to a police officer as American and Japanese visitors took a huge interest in the English 'bobby' and wanted pictures to take back home. The Americans were particularly keen to get hold of your police helmet and offered big money for it. On one occasion, I was asked by someone to pose for a photograph by Magdalen College Tower. My picture appeared on the front page of a national magazine and got me into trouble with the superintendent. No problem with the photograph, just the fact that my whistle chain was hanging down outside my tunic and looked like a toilet chain.

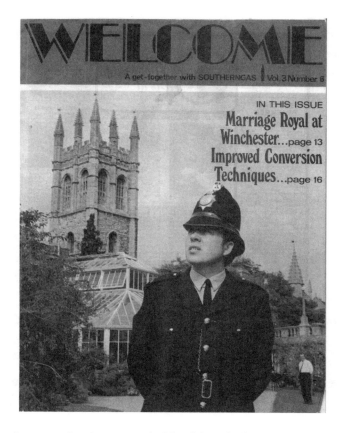

My photograph taken outside Magdalen College which featured
in a national magazine

Life on the beat in those first few months brought with it many
funny moments: for example, having to intervene when two men were
fighting over a pink scarf, and girl students streaking along the city
centre to get some attention for themselves; needless to say, I was
the first to arrive on the scene. I also well remember the evening I
was sent to rescue a girl who was wearing nothing but a smile. Being
rather naïve at the time, I was embarrassed, and used my helmet to
cover up her beauty spots. Whilst covering her up, I thought there
had been an earthquake. Traffic officers, dog handlers, police cars with
flashing blue lights and detectives all turned up at the scene and there
was me wondering why! I clearly recall one incident when another
patrol car squad arrested an elderly man for shoplifting and put him

in the back seat of the patrol car. When he got out he complained that something had bitten him on the arse, only to discover that, on entering the car, he had dropped his false teeth and had been sat on them during the journey to the police station. There are literally hundreds of funny stories like this that would fill up another book.

In those early days on the beat I remember getting grief from the local tearaways, who were streetwise and would recognise a greenhorn or new copper straight away. It gave them street cred to be the first to create some sort of disturbance to see how you'd react. I'd been warned of three such lads, who always hung around together in the city centre. This particular evening, I was standing by the bank in the city centre when I saw them in the distance. They kept staring across, so I made it my business to ask them what they were staring at and for their names. The first replied Tom, the second Dick and finally (you've guessed it) Harry. I nicked them for obstruction of the highway. Fast forward forty-five years when one of them – forget whether it was Tom, Dick or Harry – wrote to me at the BBC, asking if I would be kind enough to switch on their Christmas lights in front of local dignitaries. I duly obliged and shared some happy memories of times long gone.

Up to the mid-1960s, and prior to the introduction of personal radios, the police whistle was the only means of calling for assistance in the city centre. By the time I'd joined it was a more decorative part of the uniform and very seldom used. I recall that the only time I ever used mine was one Saturday afternoon shortly after I had finished training college. I was on foot patrol in the city centre when I saw a slip of a lass security officer wrestling with a man who had stolen a bottle of whiskey. By the time I arrived, he had run off into the nearby graveyard. I set chase and ran for all I was worth (I was able to run then; nowadays I struggle to run the bath). Eventually I managed to get hold of him and we both fell to the ground, but after much struggling it was clear he wouldn't let go of the bottle. As the radios were quite cumbersome to use, I blew my whistle full blast into his ear. He suddenly gave up the fight and collapsed. You see, it had a fearsome pitch capable of being heard by every cat and dog in a two mile radius. In fact, I'm sure I heard the headstones tremble when I blew it.

Police radios made life much easier. Pocket radiophones, huge by today's standards and hardly able to fit in your pocket, were the bee's knees when first introduced (one transmitting and one to receive). You had to be extremely careful though, as when you pressed a button the aerial would shoot out, sometimes up your nose!

There were times, of course, when a whistle or radio weren't even needed as certain police officers could put the fear of God into you just by their presence. One copper who I admired was built like a brick outhouse and kept a strict eye on his beat. To me he was the true 'Dixon of Dock Green' character in stature and temperament. His imposing figure was a deterrent to any lad with mischief on their mind and, if they spotted him, they were gone. He was an old-fashioned copper who would see children safely across the road after school. It was a sight to see him control the hundreds making their way to the car factories. He would raise his huge hand to bikes, motorists and those on foot. No one in their right mind would argue with him.

Two of the tallest police officers I've ever seen in my life joined us in Oxford. One was 6 foot 8 inches, and the other 6 foot 6 inches. You would spot them a mile away, and thankfully they were always paired off together. Passers-by just stood and stared in amazement at their size. I kept well out of their way whilst on duty and walked the other side of the road. Even with my helmet on, I only came up to their shoulders!

During my early days on the beat, there were quite a number of police substations (offices) dotted all over the area. These were used for report writing and telephone enquiries to save the need to return to the police station. Occasionally, on a wet day and nearing the end of a long shift, I would hang my raincoat and helmet out the back in the rain and go inside for a rest. Then the radio would blare out with my sergeant wanting to see me. A quick leap up and out I go

Making an arrest at a demonstration in Oxford (June 1968) – the real thing!

to put on a soaking wet raincoat and helmet. My sergeant was most impressed that I was patrolling out in the rain!

My first incident of note – which came in the first few months of my service – was a serious public disorder situation. I was crewed up in a patrol car with a colleague, when we were called to trouble inside a public house on one of the housing estates. On arrival, the disturbance had spilled out of the front of the pub and there were about twenty people fighting with each other. Our mistake was arriving too soon and not waiting for reinforcements. It was the first time in my life I was frightened. We were attacked by a large crowd of men and woman and, to make matters worse, I'd forgotten my truncheon and had split up from my colleague. I put my back to the pub wall, armed myself with a lump of wood which had been thrown at me and fought like hell. There was certainly skin and hair flying, until other coppers arrived and made arrests. I was about to leave the scene when this woman in her twenties came crashing towards me, hitting me on the head with her high heel shoe. I was battered and bruised, but lived to fight another day. Complaints came flying in against me for excessive force and violent conduct, and being armed with a lump of wood to defend myself. My reputation grew within the police and within the criminal fraternity as someone who could look after himself. I never experienced problems again.

The main offender was sentenced to two years' imprisonment and both my colleague and I received a judge's commendation. The woman who smacked me on the head got a suspended sentence. Hard to believe, but almost fifty years later she is one of my most loyal listeners on the radio.

Every police officer dreads delivering his or her first death message and I was no different. I was about three months into the job when I was told to deliver a death message to a lady who lived on her own in a flat in the city centre. Turning up in full uniform at a stranger's house is bad enough, but there is very little you can do once the message has been delivered. Contacting relatives is normally the sum total of help that can be offered. The death would have been unexpected as the deceased was her son who had been killed in a car accident in Swindon. I approached the flat with some trepidation and had mentally prepared myself. Prior to this, I made some discreet enquiries in neighbouring flats and learned she was a retired doctor, a private person who did not mix with other residents. This immediately ruled out taking a neighbour or friend with me. The bull had to be taken by the horns. I knocked on the door not sure how she would react on hearing the news. When the lady opened the door, I was nervous and anxious to deal with it quickly. She knew immediately that something was wrong. I explained as best I could the awful news, and she threw her arms around me and cried. After a cup of tea, she phoned her friend and I waited until they arrived.

Life on the beat brought a mixture of serious and light-hearted moments and was a real eye opener for me as a new recruit. Besides the regular policing activities, Oxford received a large chunk of visits from dignitaries, including royalty and heads of state from around the world. During that time I was lucky enough to see some of the most important people in the world, like President Richard Nixon of the United States and Chancellor Willie Brandt of West Germany.

SHIFT WORK

Shift work is part and parcel of an officer's life, and for me took a lot of getting used to. At Oxford there were four shifts of officers, with the same number for the smaller police station at Cowley (just outside the city and in the heart of the big Morris car factories). Each shift involved the following hours: 6am to 2pm (earlies), 2pm to 10pm (lates), and 10pm to 6am (nights). You did a week of each shift at a time.

Staff covering each shift consisted of an inspector, two sergeants and twenty-five constables. In addition, there were specialist squads, traffic officers, rural beat officers, dog handlers and operational detective officers, uncle Tom Cobley and all – a huge number of officers to deal with very little crime compared to nowadays.

Although it took me two minutes to come down the stairs for duty, the early shift was a devil. You had to parade together in a large room fifteen minutes before the hour. This parade was not only an inspection but also an opportunity to receive information about stolen vehicles, wanted persons, missing persons and crime patterns. The inspector would walk in and you had to stand up and sit down when told by the sergeant. Your truncheon, handcuffs and pocket book were produced and checked, as well as your uniform. You were then given your duty for the day and told which beat to patrol.

Two in the afternoon couldn't come fast enough. I'd head upstairs into the sitting room with the electric fire on, and would soon be asleep on the settee. Others would come in to annoy you, by blasting the television on. Another officer would arrive and clear the room out immediately when he took his shoes off. After a good afternoon's rest and supper in the canteen, the evenings were spent in the bar drinking coke and playing snooker. Sometimes the senior officers would arrive in the bar and acknowledge you. My best behaviour would then shine through, then it was back in bed by ten and up again for six in the morning. No rest for the wicked.

The late shift was my favourite and it had the same routine. You

An early picture of me in uniform

might be given different beats miles away, and the bicycle was the means of travel. During the late shift very little would happen during early afternoon, apart from the task of checking unoccupied houses and talking to people. The evenings provided an opportunity to visit the pubs and ensure they were not breaking the law by serving alcohol to underage drinkers. During quieter periods, it was also a good time to remove your helmet and sit in the back of the cinema to watch a film, all in the call of duty.

Night duty took a bit of getting used to. Trying to sleep in the day was hard but sometimes the hardest part was waking up later in the day! I remember one occasion when I went to bed after nights at ten past six in the morning and had to be awakened for ten that night for duty. I got cautioned by the inspector for being late.

Night shifts were nearly always busy, especially the first half when the pubs turned out. Trouble would often brew between the local tearaways and students from the university (town versus gown as it is locally known). Whilst still young in service and working nights, I remember one occasion when I was on foot patrol outside a club when three men came rolling out of the door scrapping for all they were worth. Any experienced copper would have let them get on with it, but not me; in I go, only for the three of them to turn on me, resulting in a protracted wrestling match on the ground. Fortunately for me, club members came to my aid until other police arrived. I never made the same mistake again.

The city centre was patrolled by about six officers on foot. The big van, called the Black Maria, was always on hand with half a dozen officers on board, its arrival on scene signalling trouble for the tearaways. This was a time when police officers took no lip from anyone and any violence towards the police was met with force. The second half of the night shift was normally uneventful. It was a time to catch up on your paperwork and take long walks on the beat, breathing in the damp crisp air. With wet and cold weather contributing to the bleakness of the streets, I allowed the beauty of the colleges to occupy my mind. I vividly recall the crunch of leaves and conkers underfoot which sounded like raw carrots being eaten.

Straying off a given beat was a disciplinary offence, punishable by a visit to the Superintendent in the morning. The rest of the night was spent checking properties along the route, door handles of shops and stopping people to ascertain where they were going, and checking their possessions. This was time-consuming as all details had to be recorded in your pocket notebook.

I soon stopped worrying about shaking hands with door knobs on my beat and, like most colleagues, I rapidly acquired a good knowledge of the best 'call-in' places where we could retreat from the cold and rain. The local hospital was a great place to drop in and enjoy a hot cup of cocoa with the nurses but, with the duty sergeant in the habit of calling up on the radio wanting to know your exact location, it was a risky journey on foot as it was a good fifteen minute walk from any of the city centre beats. This one night, everything was eerily quiet with very little happening, so I took a gamble and headed for the hospital. I was there half an hour when I heard my sergeant on the radio and I knew I was in trouble. I guessed he was back in the city centre, so I told him I was the other end of the beat some ten minutes away, to allow me time to run back. I rushed out the door only to be grabbed by the very same sergeant who proceeded to call me all the names under the sun for straying off my beat. Not for the last time he had caught me out!

Another good way to get some much needed relief from the freezing conditions was to stop off at the boiler houses in the local factories, where the nightwatchmen would be stoking coal in the boilers to heat up the machines. Like during my childhood when I used to benefit from the glow and heat from the blacksmith's furnace, it was second heaven during a long shift in icy weather to get some shelter and warmth. Again, you had to be very careful as the sergeant would be on the warpath looking for you. Sometimes we would hear him arrive, which would result in a mad rush for the exit door, leaving the telltale mug of tea or helmet behind us. One such place was the old Oxford Mail office in New Inn Hall Street, where I recall the nightwatchman put a note on the outside of the door saying no rank above constable to be allowed in during the night time. The sergeant saw the message but was as shrewd as a fox and would patiently bide his time to catch those that came out and then 'gotcha' – all hell would break loose and the resulting punishment would be walking the beat for a week in the bad weather. I did my fair share of them.

Sometimes, on icy cold nights, one of the patrol vehicles would risk picking you up and going for a spin to warm you up. I remember one occasion when one took me to the bakery and when I came in to the station the sergeant asked why I was off my beat. Concerned about the punishment that awaited, but impressed by his detective skills, I then realised that sugar from the freshly baked donuts was all down my tunic! I suppose, being a new recruit, I was a bit naive at the time, unlike the sergeant, who was 'old school' and knew every trick in the book, no doubt having done the same things himself in years gone by. I must add that, although this particular sergeant always gave the impression of being an irascible old devil, deep inside he was very funny and loved nothing better that to wind up the more innocent among us.

I soon learned to my cost that pulling pranks was part and parcel of everyday life in the police force. One night I was designated duty officer, which entailed dealing with the public at the front counter, helping out with prisoners and mortuary duties. The mortuary was situated behind the police station and had the capacity to hold about ten corpses. I had only visited there once in day light and didn't like it very much. That night I got a call from ambulance control to say they were on their way with a man who had died. My duty was to open the mortuary and ensure a space on the mortuary slab for the body. On entering, the place was in darkness and had this eerie silence about it. Switching on the lights I observed three corpses laying on slabs covered with white sheets. I was nervous, twitching and looking around. There was nobody there but me and three dead ones. Suddenly one of the sheets gently began to rise on the slab, making a wailing noise as it did so. At this point, my bum squeaked (enough detail) and I shouted for help and guidance from above. Then the white sheet dropped off, only for me to discover it was one of my colleagues. I could and should have killed him. I don't think I have ever got over this particular incident. Mind you, I can't imagine what it was like for the chap who had to lay on a slab next to two bodies in the dark of a locked mortuary!

Day shifts on Sundays, and nights, meant working on the switchboard. Nobody wanted to do it and the experienced coppers were more useful on the streets. I got allocated the job on a frequent basis, more of a punishment by the sergeant for some lapse on duty. Basically, when a call came through, you inserted different coloured cables into different coloured plug holes. You then waded through the internal telephone book and found the extension that was required. Easy, you think?

In theory, yes; in practice, no!

In reality you carried out the first part, hoping that no one else called while you were dealing with the other one as you would as likely cut them off. When this happened, you'd then wait for the ranting and raving to start when they called back. If it happened to be the chief of police you cut off, he would cast aspersions on your parenthood, schooling and anything else he could think of. Other times the chief would leave strict instructions that, although available, he wasn't to be disturbed. In short: to lie on his behalf. Not exactly ideal honesty training for coppers learning the ropes.

Sometimes, several calls came through at once, and I would inadvertently answer the least important one first, potentially causing high blood pressure or apoplexy to some senior officer. Then, of course, it was a case of throwing all the cables up in the air and praying that you hadn't connected the wrong person to the chief. On a particularly busy period it was possible to make fairly impressive looking knots of all the cables, at which point I reported sick and went home before anyone put two and two together and came up with the name Wymbs. The plus side was that things became very quiet as no one could get through on the phone. This all went on until eventually I became flustered and blew the whole bloody switchboard up!

FOOTBALL AT BOILING POINT

Away from the police, life was good. September 1968, and memories come flooding back of the All-Ireland football final between Down and Kerry. I was rostered to drive the patrol car on the late shift. I had great difficulty with the huge aerials of my old fashioned wireless and had to stick them out the window to get a reception from Dublin. I parked up in a remote area in the countryside and settled down to the commentary in spite of competing with incessant crackling noise from the wireless. Fortunately, I managed to listen to most of it with only minimal interruption from police calls. I was disappointed because

Kerry was my favourite team at the time and the lads were beaten on the day.

When I wasn't listening to sport on the radio, I was still playing it and had by now joined the local Gaelic football club in Oxford, and attended many Irish functions in the area. Football was a lot rougher in England, travel a lot further, and it also proved difficult getting time off on Sundays when the games were played. Nonetheless, I played quite a few games and was called into the Hertfordshire county team. I subsequently discovered that some of the teams were turning up to play with half their team steamed up from alcohol. The playing field was a difficult place to hold your temper while sober let alone when under the influence, and diplomacy was not in evidence. It's funny looking back now, my picture never appeared in any of the team's photographs, the reason being I was either playing when I should have been working or I was ineligible due to being a member of the police force. You see, back then, the GAA (Gaelic Athletic Association, Ireland's largest sporting organisation) placed a ban on security forces from playing Gaelic games. The authorities weren't sure at the time if this included those serving in the police force and ensured you used a different surname when playing.

A former colleague reminded me recently of one incident when I was called up to play for Oxford police at football (soccer) versus Milton Keynes. In truth, the bus was leaving and some of the better players hadn't turned up, so I was drafted in at the last minute. As was usual when two police teams met, it was a brutal game, likened to the Battle of Waterloo, with absolutely no quarter given or asked for.

My colleague recalled that we, Oxford, were giving a good account of ourselves until the ball was crossed over to him with an open goal in sight. Next thing he knows, as he rose to head the ball into the net, someone crashed into him and he experienced a sensation usually reserved for players facing the Uruguayan footballer Luis Suarez: a pair of teeth sinking into his scalp. As the world dissolved into a starry night, he made the assumption, as you might expect, that the offender was from the opposing team. Not quite. Apparently yours truly was staggering away from the scene looking like a lion that had inadvertently bitten rock rather than bone. From all accounts, my passing remark was 'I thought it was my ball'. During the vampire debacle the ball bounced harmlessly towards the goal mouth before a defender cleared it away from danger.

Unfortunately, the chaos I caused on the pitch (according to my colleague) was only matched by my ineptitude off it. After the game we entered the changing rooms which, by our standards, were opulent. They had a large bath that could accommodate the entire team, and the bath water was controlled by a large tap not reachable to those in the tub. As the bath was filling up, apparently I chose to have a shower, which led to all sorts of rumours about my manliness or lack of it. Anyway, my lovely shower buggered up the hot and cold water supply and turned the running bath water hotter. With the bath water now close to boiling point, and those in the bath unable to reach the tap, cries were made for me to come to the rescue and adjust the water temperature. With a towel modestly covering my manhood – some referred to it as a flannel – I reached over from the safety of the dry floor and started to turn the wooden collar on the handle. Unfortunately, unable to figure the bloody thing out, I made matters worse and proceeded to make the hot water hotter.

With those in the bath now tip toeing around like a scene from Swan Lake, in an attempt to avoid the encroaching boiling water, the cries fluctuated between threats and pleas until another member of the team, knowledgeable in the workings of a bath tap – red equals hot; blue equals cold – managed to re-enact Jesus walking across water, and rescue the situation. Apparently I remarked to my redder than red team mates: 'Oh, that's how it works', before ambling off to get dressed!

On a slightly more serious note, sport played an important part in the life of a police force, which is understandable as one expects the police to be fit to carry out their duties. Another factor was the public perception of police and their relationship with the local community, therefore police chiefs encouraged it. Although I didn't excel at any particular sport, I represented the Oxford police at table tennis, snooker, boxing, cross country running, and soccer. The big attraction for me was the four hours off duty to participate in those games. I suppose my greatest achievement was being selected to fight at the Royal Albert Hall in London in the European Police Boxing Championships in 1970.

Some sports were not for me, like cricket and rugby. I was utterly useless at cricket and couldn't get the hang of how to bowl and, although I enjoyed the cut and thrust of rugby, turning out for the police a couple of times when they were short, my biggest problem was understanding the rules. In one game I gathered the ball and sprinted off along the wing, only for the referee to blow the whistle and call me over to him. I was obviously offside or something. He just looked at me and said: 'It's not your game is it son?'!

PC Henry Wymbs, one of five Thames Valley policemen selected to fight in the European Police Boxing championships, at the Royal Albert Hall, London.

Me prior to my appearance at the Royal Albert Hall which appeared in the *Oxford Mail* newspaper

Chapter Six

AN OXFORD POLICE OFFICER IN THE 1970s

MEETING SALLY

Knee problems were a cause of great concern. Within a year of moving to England, I picked up an injury playing soccer and, despite my willingness to shrug off the niggling pain, I eventually succumbed and went to the doctor. It wasn't good news – I had torn my cartilage and, in the autumn of 1969, I checked in at the Nuffield Orthopaedic Hospital to have it removed. The operation was done, leg put in plaster and I had about a two week stay in hospital.

It was during my stay at the Nuffield that I first set eyes on Sally, who was a student nurse looking after me. It was her first experience of working on a ward and caring for patients, made more demanding by some cheeky Irishman requesting a bed bath! Upon leaving, I badgered her for her phone number ... which she eventually gave to me. I placed the number in my pocket and no more was said or done at that point. Some months later, I was looking for some phone numbers, and stumbled across one with the name Sally on it. Not recalling where it had come from – she obviously hadn't made that much of an impression! – I rang the number not knowing who or where I was calling. It turned out to be the nurses home at the hospital – then I remembered who it was! By chance Sally happened to be there and I was surprised to learn that she remembered me.

Anyway, I told her I was going to Ireland the next day and promised

Joan, me, Pete (back), Tina and Thomas (front)

that I would send her a postcard, which I duly did (Sally still has the postcard to this day).

I arrived home to find the place transformed. Electricity had been installed, water was now flowing from pipes to the house, and the three boys (Pete, Pat and Thomas) were in their own 'apartment' outside. Despite both my sister, Mary, and I having flown the nest (Mary left for England the year after me), the farm house was as busy as ever. My five younger siblings, Joan, John, Tina and Michael, as well as the latest edition to the Wymbs clan, baby Ann, filled the space vacated by Mary and me. Nancy and Michael had their work cut out as at that time all five children were under the age of ten! To add to the overcrowding, Granny Kate was also in residence.

During my stay I recall nosing around the back of the house but trying not to overdo it – as part of my rehabilitation from surgery, I was under strict orders from the doctors to take it easy to allow time for my knee to heal. As I reminisced about my days banging a ball against the wall, I heard Nancy shouting out of the window about not slipping on the moss. Anyway, without warning I suddenly disappeared three feet down a hole and found myself up to my chest in shite. Unbeknown to me, the moss was not only slippery, it was covering a sewage pit with a chipboard lid. Thankfully I managed to climb out with no lasting damage to my injured knee, but it was a lucky escape.

Sally was still on my mind, so I rang her when I got back to Oxford and asked her out. On our first date, I took her to a dance at Oxford Police Station, though I didn't dance much as I still had a sore leg (not that I was keen on dancing anyway)! I later discovered that I'd fractured a small bone playing football the previous day. Not the most auspicious start, you may say, but we really liked each other and started 'going out'. Sally was enjoying her nursing training and getting on well, although she did worry me a bit when she told me a story about false teeth. Apparently she had to clean the patients' false teeth and collected them all in a washing bowl. She then realised that no one knew whose teeth belonged to whom. Apparently an easy mistake to make!

I remember being nervous about meeting Sally's parents for the first time. They were, however, lovely people who adopted me as one of their own. Harrold and Phyllis had lived in Reading all their lives and had two daughters, very different from my large family. Sally's sister was already married with a baby.

By this time Sally had realised that I was the man she wanted to spend the rest of her life with – lucky Sally! She enticed me with her homemade apple tart, which tasted even better with a few cloves thrown in. Sally was steadily catching up with Nancy's tasty cooking and the old saying 'the quickest way to a man heart is through his stomach' springs to mind.

In March 1971, Sally and I got engaged, but I didn't have enough money to buy the ring. Consequently, I took two weeks' holiday working on the motorways to pay for it. Now, manual work was not my strong point, so it must have been love! I did the proper thing and

Sally and me when we got engaged in 1971

asked Sally's dad for her hand in marriage and, to my relief, he shook my hand and said 'yes – take her and her mam as well'.

Later that year Sally and I made our first trip to Ireland together and Nancy pulled out all the stops to make her welcome. It was lovely to introduce her to all my family, who by their standards behaved very well (I'm sure Nancy gagged my brother Pat to stop him from showing the family up). I believe Sally's first impression centred on how many Wymbs' there were compared to her own family, and the breathtaking scenery of sea and mountains, which made a lasting impression. The house looked splendid, as if they were expecting royalty. The only problem we encountered was when Sally asked me the way to the bathroom and I showed her into the cow barn, which had a chemical toilet in it. This was a great improvement in my eyes, but Sally wasn't too keen on the spider's webs surrounding it, especially in the dark.

Poor Sally, she got the shock of her life during that visit, when my brother Pete took her for a spin on his motorbike. The road wasn't good enough for him, so he scared the living daylights out of her by speeding like a lunatic through bog land and woods. Welcome to the Wymbs'!

Saving the hay: Cloonkeen, 1971. Sally and my Mother and Father with Tina, Ann, John and Pat

While we were there we helped with saving the hay, and everyone thought that Sally took to farming very well considering she was brought up in a town.

Me with my sister Tina on Mullaghmore Beach, 1971

POLICING IN COWLEY

After two years in Oxford enjoying working on the beat, I was transferred to Cowley police station to gain more experience. I spent the next three years there on shift work. This station covered many industrial estates, the Morris Motors car complex and large housing estates. Hard to believe now with all the closures that the five rural villages nearby each had their own police stations, with a couple of officers and a sergeant in charge of them. The transfer presented a new challenge, a diversity of policing environments, dealing with domestic incidents and early morning point duties for the thousands of workers at the factories. A whole new ball game. The brand new police station had just opened in 1966, and was similar to Oxford. I moved to live in their single men's quarters, which was a lot bigger. During that first year I had completed numerous courses, including civil defence, which was very similar to what I had learned in Cliffoney.

When I was first posted to Cowley it felt a bit of a wrench leaving all my old colleagues behind. I now had to get to know my new shift and some new sergeants. As it happened, I needn't have worried, as the transition went smoothly and I soon felt at home. I remember one of the sergeants had recently been promoted and didn't suffer fools gladly; he kept us on our toes and was difficult to read. First impressions can, of course, be deceptive and, over the next couple of years, I got to like him. Sometimes at night time, when most of us would be half asleep in the patrol cars, he would call up and ask to be picked up for a spin. He'd get me to drive to Shotover Hill, a beautiful hundred acre park overlooking the dreaming spires of Oxford, and then, on getting out of the car, would rather bizarrely produce his beloved white saxophone. I wasn't a great lover of this instrument and, to be honest, by the time he had finished playing endless tunes I would have a splitting headache. His plaintive, plangent notes soared into the night sky, sending vibrations and shock waves across the centre of Oxford from the hill tops. We would then head back in time to finish the shift, but not before he had belted out the same few lines of a song called 'Freight Train'. I must have heard it a thousand times and it was still awful. As I wrote this book word sadly came through that he had died. I will miss him, but not his damn saxophone!

Dealing with death is a traumatic experience, even for hard-nosed police officers, but having to face your first road accident fatality is daunting. I was on late shift working in the front office at Cowley ready to go home, when I heard the screeching of brakes and screaming from outside the station. I ran out, to be confronted by people seeking my help, as a man had been knocked down by a bus and was lying on the road. By then the scene was chaotic, with people crowding around the injured person. I managed to push and clear the way through, knelt down and checked his pulse to see if he was still breathing. In all honestly, the poor man was dead, but onlookers insisted I try mouth to mouth resuscitation. Those were the days before all the respiratory devices, so I had to do it. It wasn't nice, but I tried to save him by blowing air into his lungs. Afterwards I was immediately sick, but had to cover it up as police officers were role models and had to be seen as strong, and not show emotion. A doctor then arrived and certified the death.

Around this time, I moved out of police lodgings and into a large bedsit, which allowed me a little more freedom and gave me the opportunity to get away from the police environment. In an attempt to put my own stamp on the place, I remember buying a large tropical fish tank with about fifty little fish all swimming and enjoying themselves. Unfortunately, however, the enjoyment was short-lived. One evening I returned to find all the fish boiled. The tank's electronic pump had malfunctioned and, with it, came the end of my fishing days. Another time, the house nearly went up in smoke. My black and white television blew up whilst I was watching it and, in doing so, scorched the carpet and an armchair. Luckily for me I got on very well with the landlords, a lovely couple, Teresa and Allan, who became great friends. In fact, Allan was soon to be my best man.

Police work at Cowley was varied and special duties were the only occasion that overtime was paid. These duties included wrestling at

On duty at Royal Ascot

the town hall when Giant Haystacks and Big Daddy were in their prime, speedway, and the Oxford United home football games. On top of that, I also had weekends away at Ascot race meetings, Reading pop festivals, state visits and demonstrations.

Regarding the football, this was a time in the 1970s when football hooliganism was starting to rear its ugly head. Local derbies, like games against Portsmouth, Swindon and Millwall, were heavily policed. Fans would turn up drunk and fighting ensued, with police wrestling and dodging missiles. These were the days prior to protective equipment and riot shields, so there were a lot of injuries, as well as damage to cars and properties. I frequently worked in 'no man's land' between opposing fans, where we were, in effect, a human barrier. It became commonplace for fans to smuggle sharpened coins into the ground and throw them at each other, causing quite nasty injuries. The favourite coin, because of its size, was the 2 pence piece. On occasions the coins would rain down and would be picked up by the police. I remember a few times picking them up and asking the crowd if they would be so kind as to throw 50 pence pieces instead. Then there was the spitting and jeering, and missiles thrown. I dreaded this duty as supporters spat across our line and, in doing so, the police

A scorcher!

VANDALS SET fire to the goal nets at the Oxford United ground last night leaving them unusable.

Det.-Con. Tim Fleming, PC Henry Wymbs and the groundsman, Mr Leslie Bateman are pictured examining the damage, which is estimated at £30.

Police are appealing for anyone who may have seen two youths loitering near the ground at about 8 p.m. yesterday to get in touch with the St. Aldate's police station (telephone Oxford 77501).

The damage was discovered by Mr Bateman and Mr Jim Knapp, assistant secretary of the supporters' club, as Mr Knapp exercised his dog at 9 a.m. today.

Mr Bateman said there were spare nets, but they

Goal nets burned at Manor

were of the old wide mesh type which would not prevent objects being hurled through them at goalkeepers.

He said he thought newspaper must have been put under the nets to catch them alight. Grass along both goalmouths was scorched.

There is no game at the Manor today. United are away to Charlton Athletic and there is no reserves game.

A report in the *Oxford Mail* concerning vandalism at Oxford United

were covered in spit. There was no CCTV in those days and making arrests was fraught with danger. Hundreds of officers were employed both inside and outside the ground and supporters had to be escorted to the railway and bus stations. These were thugs, and their actions were reprehensible and absolutely unacceptable. This, in my mind, was a deplorable situation. All those uninhibited, riotous, inconsiderate gangs causing mayhem, and supposedly all for the love of kicking a bag of fresh air around.

Nonetheless, on the playing side it was a great time to be a copper as Oxford United played host to many of the top teams, such as Manchester United and Liverpool, in cup games. Through escorting them to the ground, I rubbed shoulders with top players like George Best, Bobby Charlton, Dennis Law, Bobby Moore, Geoff Hurst and Gordon Banks.

As well as hosting sports stars, some of the biggest names in pop music played different venues in Oxford during this time. I remember one evening, Cliff Richard was appearing in the town hall in Oxford city centre. I was a big fan of Cliff from his early days, particularly songs like 'Living Doll' and 'The Young Ones'. Unfortunately, I was unable to see him perform during his visit to Oxford as I was on duty driving a patrol car some six miles away. Anyway, keen to see him in the flesh, I took a chance and strayed off my beat into the city centre. Strictly speaking I wasn't allowed to do this, but I was ready with an excuse for being there should someone ask. I parked outside the town hall where he was due to play. Next thing I know, Cliff appeared and tried to go into the venue, only to be besieged by fans waiting outside. By luck I was in the right place at the right time and managed to rescue him by getting him into my patrol car to find the back entrance. I remember looking at him and thinking: can this be true? Only a few years earlier I was a star-struck Cliff Richard fan, but now I am his chauffeur! Anyway, I drove him to the back entry of the venue; he thanked me and I made my way back to where I should have been. What a lovely tale to tell!

MARRIAGE

Sally and I got married in Reading in June 1972, and Nancy and my brother Thomas came over and stayed for a week. Before the wedding, permission had to be granted by the police authority for us to marry, but not before rigorous checks had taken place on Sally and her family's suitability!

My stag 'do' was a relatively low key affair: a pub in Oxford where I was forced to 'down' a yard of ale, all in one go, from a peculiar shaped glass. I'm glad I'd reached maturity before the fashion for ramping up the pre-wedding ritual to long weekends in Magaluf.

Sally and I moved into a police house in Oxford. It was large, with a huge side garden, but it had no central heating and the metal windows would steam over with condensation on damp days. It also had an old fashioned larder big enough to put a donkey in. I immediately got to work on the garden and grew a variety of vegetables, including cabbages as big as footballs, carrots, parsnips, and spuds (the Irish staple!). At the time the police would either grant you a rent allowance or provide a married couple with a house. Prior to this, officers had to be in the job for a number years before they were allowed to buy their own. We were lucky, the rules changed and six months later we bought the house and lived there until 1980.

At the time we did not have a washing machine, and visited the local launderette on a weekly basis. We also changed cars, and were now the proud owners of an old banger, a 1953 Ford Consul, with column changing gears and a radio which sparked when switched on. The Consul took half an hour to warm up, and poor Sally showed extreme courage and bravery by using it for work. By now Sally had opted out of nursing due to clashing with my shift work, and had a job as a clerical officer with health and social security.

During the early 1970s the general UK economy was in a bit of a slump and there was high inflation. Remember this was shortly before the introduction of the 'three day week', when electricity was rationed and power cuts came into force, meaning that television had to close down by 10.30pm. In those days the majority of people weren't able to buy a television and had to rent them from companies like Radio Rentals. A sharp contrast to the way we live today, with credit easily available and twenty-four hour television the norm.

It was a time of 'make do and mend', and both Sally and I had to be quite creative at times. I remember spending a long time making a garden fence out of floorboards. The boards all had long bent nails in them and cut the hands off me pulling them out. I didn't have all the mod cons of electric saws, or the throw away type you see nowadays.

Our wedding day, June 1972, with Thomas, Nancy and Sally's
mum and dad

The old rusty saw had been left in the shed when we moved into the house and probably came from the Second World War. The few teeth left in it wouldn't cut butter and I had to saw about eighty long boards with it. I'm sure I still have some of the blisters left on my hands to this very day. Meanwhile, Sally made her own curtains, and hand-me-downs from family were welcome, plus, although I moaned about it, my experience in preparing and repairing cars paid dividends. What's more, Sally's dad, an electrician, was brilliant and installed central heating for us. He also showed me how to wire up power and light cables without blowing myself up!

Sally's parents often came and stayed for weekends, helping to create flower borders and tidying up the garden. I have fond memories of us enjoying a game of cards in the evenings, which took me back to my days in Cloonkeen and reminded me that, although I was far away from my family in Ireland and missed them dearly, I was very lucky to benefit from the warmth and generosity offered by my adopted family.

Away from married life I was still enjoying singing and, at about that time, I formed a duo with my mate, Charlie McGlynn. We called ourselves the 'Bionic Men' (much to Charlie's embarrassment). He knew nothing about this name until he turned up for a gig in a public house. You see, when the pub booked us we had yet to decide on a name and so I had to think quickly. The Bionic Man was a name off the TV at the time and so, for some reason, came to mind when I was asked.

We received rave reviews from people who knew nothing about music. It was difficult for me because, for starters, I didn't have permission from the police, which I needed, and secondly, I was bumping into villains who jeered at me – I wasn't sure if it was the singing or the police factor they disliked most. We did, however, get fifteen quid each – a lot of money in those days. After a couple of years and with no stardom in sight we packed it in. I still see Charlie to this day – lovely fella.

Meanwhile, the Irish scene in Oxford was quite vibrant, with hundreds employed in the car factories and in construction. Certainly in the post-war decades the proportion of Irish emigrants who disappeared into poverty and destitution was quite high. There wasn't much for them at home and there was a promise of better abroad, but unfortunately sometimes reality falls short of the promise.

A lot of the Irish mixed with their own people, so it was like home from home in one sense. It was, however, lonely for those that would return to their one room bedsit with no family close by and very little comfort (maybe no television or radio). It was nice to meet someone from home and chat about which county you came from. Inevitably the pub was the main meeting place and, of course, for some alcohol anaesthetised their loneliness and despair. In the main, Irish people got on with their lives, were hardworking, honest and reliable.

Oxford didn't have an Irish club of its own but the local halls provided nights to remember, with big bands from Ireland (especially during Lent) taking centre stage. The majority of Irish people in Oxford were from Mayo, Wexford, Galway or Laois. I got to know many and have remained friends with a number of them all my life.

Interestingly I only ever met a couple of folk living in Oxford who had originated from my area, and funnily enough one of them, Frank McHugh, was with me at school during my 'tech' days. I seem to recall whilst at school both of us were sent on 'gardening leave' during the music sessions, weeding the turnips and spuds. I'm not sure why Frank was with me, but certainly my leave of absence would have been for some kind of misbehaviour. Frank continues to live in Oxford and is a very successful businessman. His brother Colm, who I was also friendly with, sadly passed away some years ago in Oxford.

COMMUNITY BEAT OFFICER

Things changed for me in 1973 when I was offered the job of community beat officer for an area in Oxford that included the Iffley Road running track on which Roger Bannister ran the first sub-four-minute mile in 1954. The dwellings were multi-occupied, with hundreds of students. With it came a variety of challenges: drug taking, noise, traffic problems and complaints from the public.

I was given my own police cycle to patrol the area, a really positive experience, meeting all the friendly shopkeepers, pub landlords, sampling the delicious food from the restaurants and engaging with university students to keep them on the straight and narrow.

My sergeant trusted me to carry out my duties and we would only meet up once or twice a week. The bulk of my work was taken up with serving summons and following up enquiries on missing persons, minor thefts (like milk from doorsteps), traffic accidents and untaxed motor vehicles. It was known for the label of a Guinness bottle to be displayed on a windscreen as a tax disc. I seem to recall this happening when driving the minivan at Maye's Motors! I really enjoyed my time patrolling this lovely little patch.

I suppose the most bizarre incident of my career occurred one evening when I got a call to a break-in at a high-rise block of flats. The door was opened by a lady, stark naked, who promptly invited me

'Striking nurses on the march', Me policing a demonstration in 1974

upstairs to see the damage for myself. Times like this I wish I was born lucky and not good-looking. What was I to do? I always tried to defuse a tricky moment with some wisecrack. I then heard a man's voice, which somewhat eased the situation. Little else could I do than follow her upstairs. By then, I didn't know whether I was coming or going in the confusion. Upstairs sat a man, stark naked, reading a book. I subsequently learned that they were part of a nudist colony. As you can imagine, I didn't know where to look as I took their lengthy statement.

Around this time a new inspector arrived on the shift, a strict but fair disciplinarian who led from the front. He was a devout Roman Catholic who made sure whilst on duty that I went to church on Sunday mornings, even pulling me away from urgent police work. To ensure I looked the part, he would even loan me his jacket.

The Sunningdale agreement on Northern Ireland took place in nearby Berkshire just before Christmas in 1973. It was one of the coldest months for a long time, and I'll never forget standing outside for days in the wind and rain. It was the longest and most boring week in my life – give me thinning turnips back in Cloonkeen any day. The politicians would wander around the grounds and make conversation, including John Hume and Gerry Fitt, who always took the time to speak to me when they passed by.

In August 1974 I found myself in Windsor for a few days because a group of anarchists and others decided to hold a free music festival in the Queen's back garden. By the sixth day it was agreed that enough was enough. We paraded at an unearthly hour and were transported to the campsite, which was quiet at the time. Officers then went from tent to tent warning people that they had fifteen minutes to vacate the site. They were not happy bunnies.

An hour later all hell broke loose in Windsor town centre, when the group, now in their hundreds and fronted by another 'rent a mob', unwisely took the police on. Hand to hand fighting was everywhere, with the demonstrators coming off second best. Amazed foreign tourists with cameras were told by police not to take photographs and ran for cover. The following day, all the national papers headlined the story with 'The Battle of Windsor' and carried pictures of fallen anarchists with coppers standing over them. To make matters worse, a brutality petition was handed to the chief of police. My picture appeared on the front page of *The Sun* newspaper.

A further example of how something that is initially fairly innocuous can easily get out of hand was when I was dealing with someone with no lights on their bicycle. I was in a patrol car one evening when we pulled this man over and advised him of the danger, but there would be no summons on this occasion. Suddenly he went berserk, throwing his bike to the ground and calling us all names under the sun. In the ensuing struggle three of us ended up in a garden, knocking over a large brick wall. The newspapers the following day captured the severely dented bike and the damaged brick wall, which resulted in a protracted court case and heavy fines.

Meanwhile exams were again on my mind. In 1973, I had foolishly sat the national sergeant's examination without studying enough first. I failed the exam and got such poor marks that I was hauled up before the Superintendent. Mind you, I wasn't the only one. Only nine out of five hundred in the force passed, resulting in the introduction of stricter guidelines, whereby failure would only be accepted if you provided proof of at least a year's study before the exam. With some apprehension, in the summer of 1974 I decided to give it another go and enlisted on a twelve-month correspondence course of home study which had exams at the end of each month. The course cost a lot of money and, with Sally's support, I got down to the task in hand.

The laughing policeman

When not studying I was busy meeting sporting world champions. I had always loved the game of draughts, but up to that point had only ever played at a beginner's standard, seeing one move ahead. One day, whilst working on the beat, I got talking to an elderly man outside his house and the conversation turned to hobbies. I was truly amazed when I learned that he was a world champion at draughts and that he was at that time playing a match against a chap who was living in Russia. Now remember this was 1974, many years before online gaming came along, so you may rightly ask how on earth he managed to play an opponent who was taking his turn from his armchair in Russia. Quite simple, in those days each move from each player was sent, not by the click of a mouse, but by telegram. It took the best part of a year to complete each game. Amazing really to think how things have changed.

Anyway, after a long discussion, I couldn't miss the opportunity of getting a few tips from a world champion, so I took the plunge and asked him to teach me. We played a couple of matches and, unsurprisingly, the contest was short lived! He basically wiped the floor with me after just a couple of moves; not to show off, mind you, but just to see how good or bad I was. From that point I learned the game from scratch over a period of years and eventually became quite good, challenging everyone in sight, usually for a small wager. I always carried the draughts set with me whilst at work and, if the truth be known, made a few bob along the way.

One incident still etched in my brain is when I was crewed up with a Scotsman on night duty. He always wanted to drive the patrol car, as he believed my driving was so atrocious even riding a bike should be off-limits (fair comment). Anyway, at about two in the morning, things were relatively quiet and my Scottish colleague took me to this 'posh' place with an indoor swimming pool. The owners were away for the weekend and had given him permission to use the pool. Having parked the car well away from the house and streetlights, so as not to cause suspicion among the neighbours, we entered via a side door using a torch to show us the way. We then proceeded to change in the porch, leaving all our uniform on a chair. Being diligent coppers, we took the car keys and radio in with us just in case we got a call.

Everything was going swimmingly (pardon the pun) until the dreaded radio went into overdrive. To our horror, someone had seen movements in the pool and had called the police. A bit of a dilemma: what do we do? As if things weren't bad enough, they were just about to get worse. On checking our clothes, we noticed that, although the top half of our uniform was still on the chair, our trousers were missing. Panic set in: no trousers, no underpants (as they were soaking from the swimming), and not even a towel to wrap around us.

We put the uniform on (minus trousers) and deliberated. Although, in theory, we could leave the building, two coppers walking out of a building at gone two in the morning without trousers was sure to attract some attention! In addition, contacting the station wasn't an option as we would have some awkward questions to answer.

To buy ourselves some time we answered the radio and told the control room we were on our way. Then ... wouldn't you know it – in walks one of our mates with the trousers. Unbeknown to us he had seen us in the pool and hidden them, the sod!

CID AND A NEW BABY

The year 1975 was a momentous one for me. In January, I passed the selection board to join the criminal investigation department (CID). This meant a gruelling twelve-week detective training course at Scotland Yard once you had proved your capabilities on the ground. Although it may sound glamorous, this work entailed a mountain of paperwork, observation and intelligence gathering. You knew the criminals and the crimes they'd committed – that was the easy part – now you had to prove it. In those days criminals were arrested on what we called 'a wing and a prayer' or a 'fishing expedition' in the hope they would admit their part without having to resort to real police work in order to prove the case.

The good criminal would just acknowledge you, stare at a spot on the wall and say nothing. It was very frustrating as some of those people were guilty of dreadful crimes. The good and bad cop scenario would then be put to the test. I was always the nice guy and, if that didn't work, the big ugly brute of a detective would try and work his magic by thumping the desk and demanding answers. Sometimes it worked. Other times it didn't.

The great strength of the police back then was that we worked as a team and showed a willingness to tackle any problem. Most of them would go through hell and high water to a call for assistance. The canteen would empty as well as every office.

There were three teams of detectives at Cowley police station. Each team had one detective sergeant and four detective constables, and two teams would usually double up. Sharing intelligence was vital to access the information coming through. Among the teams, there were some 'glory' boys more interested in keeping information secret

Me as a young detective in 1975

to justify their own worth and look good on appraisals but, in the main, those characters were few and far between.

We often faced the most harrowing sights: burglaries, robberies, drownings, suicides, shootings and the faces of those left behind. Human beings at their worst. You may rightly ask, 'why bother with this type of work?' I guess deep down I have always believed in the value of public service and the importance of upholding the law. I think it helped that I always had the ability to laugh at myself and of course the bit of 'craic' thrown in (not the happy pill).

Burglary is a crime victims fear greatly. Not only does the thief steal your precious and personal belongings, but they also invade your privacy. Most burglars are opportunists and commit their crimes during the summer months when windows and doors are left open. Mind you, I also saw my fair share of them in the lead up to Christmas, when the thief would simply prize open the top transom window, put his hand through, open the large side window and climb in.

One prolific burglar (known very well to the police) would use this method of entry into a complete row of maybe ten terraced houses, and escape with hundreds of pounds in coins deposited in pre-payment electric metres. On one particular occasion, which I attended on Christmas day morning, he had to step over a visiting 'granny' asleep in a spare bed by the window, unscrew the meter in the kitchen, and then feed the turkey to the dog to keep it quiet. You couldn't make it up!

The same burglar was forever being stopped in the street, searched and arrested, but was never in possession of items implicating him in crime. Having been seen lifting man hole covers in the streets, covert observations were mounted in an attempt to catch him. He was as cute as a fox and stored his tools and ill-gotten gains in the nearest drain hole until the heat was off and he felt safe enough to return, dressed in a workman's uniform, to collect his bounty. He was eventually caught and spent many years in prison and, on release, would resume his old habits once more. Unfortunately this is not that uncommon in the criminal world. Some of the criminals I encountered would spend their entire life in and out of prison and act in a similar fashion to a bad gambler. If you're a good gambler, you know when to stick and when to twist. They didn't know when to stick and so ended up getting onto a roulette wheel they were unable to get off (to continue the gambling thread).

Quite a few houses had pre-payment gas meters, but they were a little more difficult to break into because of the fear of damaging the gas pipe in the process. Nevertheless, for some villains it proved a challenge they couldn't resist. One incident stands out when we were called to the casualty department at the local hospital to investigate the circumstances of a man who was admitted with burns to his face and hands. On chatting to him he gave us some 'cock and bull' story of being a gas fitter who had accidentally burned himself. He was not the brightest bulb in the lamp, in fact he was as thick as Bisto, and we soon unravelled the mystery. He admitted that in his endeavour to get to the coins, he had used a blow lamp to burn the lock off the meter and in doing so caused an explosion which nearly blew the house up as well as himself. You meet one every day ...

Another despicable crime committed by burglars was nicking lead off church roofs. On one occasion, when questioned, neighbours reported they had failed to raise the alarm as the culprits were wearing fluorescent jackets and looked 'official'. The same response was given by a vicar who had been duped by a couple of dodgy roofers. 'You can't go around assuming that anyone who wears a fluorescent jacket is an angel,' was my comment to the vicar. 'Bless them, they must have been very hard up,' he said. 'Bless them my arse,' was my instant reply.

Compared to how things work now, policing was far less professional back then. For instance, I have known occasions when carrying out a raid on a property would involve the police turning up with sledge hammers to break down the door, only to find out that they had smashed the front door of some innocent old lady's property by mistake.

Executing search warrants was a common occurrence on CID and often led to many comical events. I recall one search involving a grandmother, who stood in the same spot in the corner of the room whilst we were searching for stolen jewellery. She refused to move until I gave her a nudge and there under her feet lay a huge quantity of stolen rings and watches. Another time, we got a tip-off about stolen electrical gear buried in the back garden of a house, which had a vegetable patch. We had to dig the potatoes up to find a large metal container hiding ten new toasters, half a dozen kettles and several top of the range cutlery sets. Del Boy himself would have been proud!

One of the funniest incidents (although it may not sound it at first) occurred when three ferocious dogs were let loose on us as we tried to enter a house. It was one of those houses where you wiped your feet on the way out. We were aware of the animals beforehand and so had originally intended to arm ourselves with two fire extinguishers to frighten them off. Our sergeant, however, loved dogs and decided that he had the skills required to handle them without using the foam. He sat down and gently coaxed one of them over to him, when suddenly another of man's best friends jumped up and bit him on the nose (I was grabbed by the mad dog too!). We were in absolute stitches, and in a different way so was he – he had to have two on his face. He eventually saw the funny side (I think).

I had my own bad experience with dogs, but this time without any physical injury, I'm pleased to say. It occurred when I was on duty at some dubious CID celebration or other, at one of the less fashionable pubs. Come midnight, I stumbled out, making my way to the main road. Not sure where I was going or what I was doing, I saw a police dog van and waved it down. The driver instantly recognised me, offering me a lift home. He had a passenger in the front seat and had just dropped the dog off at the kennels. I got in the back and arrived home safely. In I went, to be met by Sally, sniffing her nose and pointing to the brown substance on my trousers and shirt. As you can guess, the dog van had not been cleaned out!

Observations were a pain. Although police work can be very interesting and entertaining, five hours in the back of a van looking through a keyhole window on a cold winter's night does not make for good television viewing. One occasion I'll never forget was an observation outside a public house, when I was teamed up with a female colleague. The public picnic area in front of the pub provided an ideal setting for a courting couple. It was a bright sunny day and we were both in shorts. The target was likely to come along, park his car and enter the pub with his girlfriend. Once this happened, other officers would be alerted and arrest the suspect. You follow me so far?

Ready for action (as it were), I was laid on my stomach facing the pub, while my female colleague was sitting up reading a book. Then without warning a sudden pain hit me in the nether regions. I looked down to discover I was being eaten alive by fire ants, which had somehow got into my underpants. Obviously I couldn't scream out as it would attract attention. I was in agony, wriggling around to get rid of them. Then, my colleague came to my rescue by shouting, 'get them off!' That was the first – and only – time in my life a woman ever said those immortal words to me. She wrapped a rug around me and I did get them off. One of the worst experiences in my life, and to make matters worse the target never showed up!

Back on the home scene at the end of July 1975, Duncan arrived. We were absolutely thrilled, a bonny little boy. I suppose parents would agree with me that the birth of a child is the most important event in your life. Duncan was born at the John Radcliffe Hospital, Oxford. Life for us changed. I was working long hours and, with no family around to help, Sally had to cope on her own.

Meanwhile, throughout that year I was kept busy with the Sergeant's correspondence course, which was a tough slog and I had to be very self-disciplined; at least two hours' a day for twelve months is a mighty long time. By the end of the course I was exhausted. I remember on the final exam day being surprised at the hundreds of officers like me turning up for the day of reckoning. It was an all-day sit-in with three different two-hour examinations. I, like all the other offices, then had to wait patiently for the results to come through.

In September I got the news that I had prayed for. I'd passed the exam. I was over the moon. The course had been tough and there is no doubt that without Sally's help and persuasion I would have never made it. Getting the results brought back memories of how I had felt back in Sligo eight years earlier when I had got the invitation letter for the police interview. At least this time I wouldn't have to train from scratch and there wouldn't be the ordeal of height and sight tests!

Looking back, I think the news of my results came as a shock to a lot of other coppers, as many didn't believe I was capable of passing. As it happened, only eight out of five hundred and fifty officers in the Thames Valley got through. I later learned others followed the same route as me with correspondence courses.

Back in my post and by the end of the year my work load was huge. Every time I answered the phone, I picked up a job. It would have been very easy to go under. I had whole cases to deal with, from start to finish, and had responsibility for preparing the evidence to a point where the case went to court. Despite the hectic schedule, I was determined to get the detective course behind me and try for promotion to sergeant. Christmas came and went without Duncan knowing anything about it. He was, by then, a big boy with a head of curly hair. Sally took to motherhood and coped very well.

In March 1976, I went off to Scotland Yard for twelve weeks for the CID course, leaving Sally on her own to look after Duncan. I travelled home from London every other week. At the same time exams were not over for me. By that point, police exam systems had changed, with constables being allowed to sit the inspector's exam before being promoted to sergeant. Once again, study took over as I worked towards the inspector's exam.

After the twelve weeks I was back home again, pleased to get through the course and feeling quietly confident about the inspector's exam. A few weeks later I was delighted to hear that I had passed it, which was a lovely feeling as I could now stand up to the chief of police and say 'I passed the same exams as you'. Of course, passing all of these exams was no guarantee of promotion, as I was soon to find out.

WORKING FOR PROMOTION

1977, and Stephen was born in March of that year. He was much smaller than Duncan, who by now was proving to be a handful in more ways than one. The two boys brought much warmth and excitement into our home. The energy and joy that children bring to families and grandparents is wonderful. Despite the latest arrival,

Double trouble, 1978

I was still expected to work long hours with no overtime. Over the course of the next couple of years Duncan was into everything and, with a baby brother now in tow, he encouraged him to follow suit, delving into kitchen cupboards and causing mayhem. Both of them were a real handful in those days, and trying to keep the house in one piece was difficult. Like many families at the time, it was hard as, when Stephen came along, both of them were in nappies and we didn't have the disposable ones that are taken for granted nowadays.

When Duncan was a baby we were very adventurous (for us) and bought a small caravan. I even made a cot which fitted into the furniture. When Stephen arrived we bought a bigger one, but I wasn't too keen on towing it – anyone who knows my driving will know that reversing is not my strongest point. We had to try not to make a wrong turn otherwise we were in big trouble! Holidays in those days were usually a week away to Devon or the Dorset coast.

The beginning of 1978 saw the arrival of a newly promoted detective sergeant to supervise us. He was a really nice man, with a cheerful disposition and a broad outlook on life. Computers had not yet been introduced, and all paperwork and records were stored manually. One evening, I was called into his office to discuss some ongoing crime enquiry, when I noticed he was in the process of compiling an index of some sort. I told the other members about my discovery and we came to the conclusion that he was a bit too keen for our liking and we better watch out. When he went out, we checked the index only to discover it was a list of his racing pigeons! One of the best detective sergeants I ever worked for.

By now I was thinking of promotion and keeping my nose clean of complaints from villains. This was an occupational hazard for me. The villains would get their heads together and complain about incivility, threats, not adhering to police rules and everything else under the sun. In fairness, some of the complaints may have been justified.

Encouragingly, I was made acting detective sergeant on another team of detectives to gain experience for any forthcoming promotion boards. The move proved a challenge, as two of the detectives were of the 'old school'; known throughout the criminal world as hard men. My acting role was to investigate the more serious crimes and closely supervise the team under me.

Some evenings, as part of our work, I would join them for a drink in some dingy old pub on a rough housing estate. After a few pints, finger waving began when the two detectives made gestures to other so called hard men in a corner. I was a dwarf compared to my two mates and, not only did I not fancy a good kicking, I didn't want any bother to thwart my attempt at promotion. Then came the scrapping, with 'muggins' joining in, rolling all over the floor, and customers shouting police brutality. Uniform coppers then turned up in their vans and whisked the baddies away. After a dusting down, we went back to base, wondering what the hell that was all about. This was the way things were back then.

Other times we worked as 'spotters' at football matches or demonstrations, when offenders would be identified and nicked on their way out. Tricky situations sometimes developed, your identification blown, and maybe your picture would appear in the criminals' equivalent of a rogues' gallery.

In 1978 the promotion board arrived at long last, when I was formally interviewed by a panel of three senior officers from other districts. Promotion boards were only held when vacancies were anticipated and if you were successful you were then placed into a pool of qualified officers to be offered a position. Before any of this occurred, you had to be selected as suitable by your own chief superintendent. The interview lasted forty minutes and was quite difficult. I fluffed it, with no reason given for failure. Ah well ... another time perhaps? As it happened, I had to wait another twelve months for the next promotion board to come up. The interview was held at Police Headquarters and I remember the panel consisted of an assistant Chief Constable, a Chief Superintendent and a Chief Inspector, all unknown to me. It was basically a question and answer interview, with the odd police scenario thrown in on how you would deal with certain incidents. This time the interview seemed to go well and I walked out feeling quietly confident. Weeks rolled by until the letter finally fell through the letterbox. You would know straight away if you had passed before even taking the letter out, as a green slip of paper meant pass and a white slip meant fail. Out came the green slip … Great news! It was time to celebrate and have a couple of drinks, which I duly did, but not before a hair-raising moment for me in court.

Unfortunately, earlier in the year I'd investigated a case which was up for trial the day I got word of my promotion. However, the offender ended up pleading guilty, which was a great result – no need to give evidence. Lunchtime came, had a drink or two. Then, to my horror, I was unexpectedly called back to court to stand in the witness box to give details to the judge. Would he smell alcohol? I was certain the vapour from my breath would reach him. There goes my promotion, up in smoke. Fortunately, I managed to get through it by trying not to speak in his direction! Another close shave.

On the home front, although with two young boys it was hard work to travel to Ireland, especially in winter, we decided to go to

Christmas in Ireland, 1979

Sligo for Christmas in 1979. This was the first and only time I spent Christmas in Sligo with Sally and the boys. Off we went on the ferry from Holyhead to Dun Laoghaire, a long journey at the best of times, but in those days made ten times worse by having an old car and having to negotiate appalling roads across Ireland. The journey from Oxford to Holyhead took about eight hours, then five hours on the ferry crossing, and five hours to Sligo. Looking back, we didn't have a mobile phone and if we had broken down – reasonably likely, given our old banger – we would have had no chance of an emergency call out. Happily, we made it. The home layout in Cloonkeen had changed again since our last visit, with a new kitchen extension now built at the back; however, the turf in the range was still burning strong. I warmly remember Sally and the boys being treated like royalty as we sat down on Christmas Day to eat the festive trimmings surrounded by what seemed like the whole Wymbs clan. The boys were young at the time and enjoyed being spoilt by the family. Even Santa Claus paid them a visit!

I remember that when I used to return home I was so proud as Nancy would have a lovely photo of me pride of place on the sitting room wall. However, little did I know, until recently, that the picture came down as soon as I left for the boat back to England to be replaced by one of my sister Mary, who would be next to visit!

The trip home to Cliffoney was a good time to enjoy a cup of Barry's tea, a bag of Tayto crisps and many other treats I was not able to purchase in my adopted city of Oxford. I always crammed as much of these brands as possible into my suitcase ahead of my return journey, hoping to savour the sweet taste of home for just a little longer.

A few months before our visit, the world's media had descended onto the seaside resort of Mullaghmore, only a few miles from my birthplace, due to an incident which had a profound impact on the English royal

My brother Thomas is introduced to Prince Charles in
Mullaghmore in 2015

family. Looking out to the west of Mullaghmore lies the ancient
monastic island of Innismurray, which has been uninhabited since just
after World War Two. Closer inland stands Classiebawn Castle. The
castle was built in the mid-19th century by Lord Palmerston, a former
Prime Minster of England. It later became the home of Lord Louis
Mountbatten, great grandson of Queen Victoria. His whole family,
daughters, sons-in-law, and the entire clutch of grandchildren with
nannies would spend the month of August each year at the castle.
Mountbatten felt at ease and would visit the local shops, talking to
customers and walking along the harbour. In 1971, when Sally first
visited Mullaghmore, Mountbatten came walking past us on his way
to his boat, with no obvious security around him.

In August 1979, Mountbatten's boat was blown up by the IRA off
the coast of Mullaghmore. He was killed, together with three others,
sending shockwaves around the world. In May 2015, Prince Charles
and his wife, Camilla, arrived in Mullaghmore for a deeply personal
pilgrimage to the spot where his great uncle Lord Mountbatten was
killed. Hundreds of people cheered the royal couple as they mixed
freely with locals and visitors alike. My brother, Thomas, who worked
at Classiebawn Castle in the seventies, was one of the chosen few to
meet the royal couple. As a result, Thomas's picture with the royal
couple appeared worldwide on television and in national newspapers.

Chapter Seven

AN OXFORDSHIRE DETECTIVE

POLICING IN DIDCOT

Even though I had passed my exams and conquered the promotion board, I had to wait for a vacancy to come up and finally, in the spring of 1980, I was promoted to uniform sergeant at Didcot. I had initially been offered a position in the market town of Chesham in Buckingham, a very expensive area for housing. I accepted the job, but we struggled to sell our house and six months later I was offered Didcot, which I accepted. On the home front, a few months later, in June, we moved to our present house in a more rural setting, which we loved, and still do.

Policing at Didcot was a real eye opener – a huge rural area with many beautiful villages. The town was dominated by huge cooling towers from the power station which powered up some 2 million households. Apart from the towers, the area had a number of massive atomic energy laboratories known the world over. What's more, the psychiatric hospital was situated near the main motorway, and the fast flowing river Thames and the highspeed train to London. (No need to tell you the police were kept busy with many horrific incidents with the patients.)

On my arrival at Didcot, I immediately decided to 'set out my stall' by being a no-nonsense sergeant and change my style of policing

Outside our new home, 1980

away from the 'happy go lucky chap' on CID. I firmly believed in the zero tolerance approach to public order offences and dealt firmly with offenders. I also encouraged high visibility policing in previously known trouble spots. I believe this approach worked.

The station itself was relatively new, with a Superintendent in charge, three shift systems, a station sergeant and some uniform carriers who should have been put out to grass long ago. I now had to get back to my books and learn the law on diseases of animals, poaching, coursing, firearms, land disputes, entertainment licences and all sorts of weird bylaws and fishing rights. On my shift were a few 'old sweats' that'd seen it all before and a new sergeant wasn't going to change their habits.

Rural policing brought its own difficulties, with many neighbourly quarrels, and at times I had to act as a sponge to absorb what I was told by gossip mongers. The day shifts could be boring when nothing much happened, but when it did, there weren't enough of us to deal with any given situation. Late evenings and the start of the night shift, especially at weekends, could be busy. With four coppers and myself to police a huge area, it meant trouble in one area would tie up a couple of cars twelve miles away from a pub fight. Not like the city, when a call would result in twenty coppers arriving on site in an instant.

During my time at Didcot I learned to survive by not rushing into public order situations. One village was big horse racing country and, come the weekend, the jockeys – five foot nothing of them – would fight like cat and dog (or should that be horse and pony?). I would take my time getting to the pub and then pick up the pieces, with no one complaining.

Another pub had a reputation for late night drinking. We knew it was going on, and would turn up with blue lights flashing. Then the inevitable stampede of drinkers exiting through the rear gardens, which was a sight to behold. It was always difficult raiding a pub with only a

Nancy with me in our garden in Oxford shortly after I got promoted

couple of officers and so, providing it wasn't an ongoing problem and there was no trouble, the landlord would be spoken to, which usually resolved the matter. The complaints of late night drinking very often came from wives or other landlords.

Like all towns and villages, Didcot had its known trouble-makers. On my arrival to the station I had been warned about one particular man who had a dislike of the police, and under no circumstances should he be approached without back-up. Then, one night, a call came through for immediate assistance to a flat where this man was threatening neighbours. All the other officers were busy, just leaving me and a young policewoman to attend. She was scared, but what could we do?

Anyway, we arrived near the flat and spoke to some neighbours, who didn't help matters by telling us that the last time the man was arrested it took five coppers and a police dog to subdue him and get the handcuffs on. As we got closer to the man's front door, I could hear Irish rebel songs blaring out of his open window, and thought, here goes ... I was then confronted by a gorilla, one of the biggest men I've ever seen, tattoos everywhere. He stepped forward. 'Where's the riot squad, you pig? And a bloody sow as well,' he growled menacingly. By now, I was concerned and my colleague was confused: 'who's the sow?' she said. 'You dear,' I replied. I tried to make conversation above the loud music by referring to the songs being played. He seemed to calm down, once he detected my Irish accent. By now sirens were blaring, and blue flashing lights everywhere. I ordered them away to prevent him from getting more agitated and, after a while, we entered the flat and had a cup of tea with him. Although he was big he actually had a heart of gold and falsely presented himself as a 'hard' man.

People with mental health problems quite often came into contact with the police and at times were very unpredictable and difficult to handle. One evening I was called to a hospital as a lady had locked herself in the toilet and refused to come out. I'm not sure why the staff didn't sort it out, but times were different then, and the police were called to every little incident. After a lot of sweet-talking, she came out smiling and sat down with me. We both had a cup of coffee, when suddenly without any warning she threw the cup of coffee over me. Lucky for me, it had gone cold, so no lasting damage to my handsome face.

One thing I dreaded was a road accident involving police vehicles, when the sergeant became investigating officer, having to submit a large file of papers to the director of public prosecutions for their advice. For some reason coppers did their best to crash their police cars when I was on duty, causing me unjust stress and relentless arm waving, cursing, swearing and threats of all kinds. I had no problem with all the paperwork, but the scene plan had to be precise and to scale. My 'tech' and drawing days came back to haunt me. Perhaps I should have had more kicks up the backside to help me at times like this. My one saviour was an officer who knew of my weakness. He was the plan drawer for some serious incidents in Thames Valley Police. My – or shall I say his – plans were so good that they were mentioned in dispatches as a fine example to other officers. Great result.

One incident I recall very well was when one of the sergeants took a disliking to the inspector, who had gone away on holiday for a fortnight. It was during one of the hottest summers ever. The inspector always locked his office to prevent others riffling through his papers, but a duplicate key was found and something placed in his office drawer, door locked. A week later, an inexplicable and rather unpleasant smell pervaded the station, until the source of it was discovered. Some mackerel fish had been placed in the inspector's drawer! The office had to be fumigated at a cost to the police authority, and a superintendent from another area was drafted in to investigate. We were all interviewed under caution in an effort to find the culprit but, although it was common knowledge among the staff who did the dirty deed, without evidence it just remained a 'fishy' tale!

A fatal traffic accident involving a child was one of my worst fears and in my early career I had managed to avoid having to deal with one, until, of all times, one Christmas Eve. I was due to finish early when I got a call to a serious car accident just outside Didcot involving a child. When I arrived, people were crowding around and trying to help. My heart stopped: a little boy aged six had stepped out in front of a car while walking with his mother; her baby in the pram. The little boy was dead. My son Duncan was the same age at the time. It could have been him. I cried on the road, thinking 'there but for the grace of God'. Of all the horrible things I have seen in my life, this incident still haunts me to this very day.

THE MINERS' STRIKE

After a couple of years as patrol sergeant, I got the job as station sergeant at Didcot, mainly due to my knee problems, which curtailed my abilities to get involved in patrol work. The job was nine to five with weekends off, which was good, but the work was quite testing, with responsibilities ranging from custody, rural beat officers, running the station, court work and preparing duties. The duties took up a lot of my time and was a most onerous task, which led to me being labelled the 'Tippex king' (Tippex being the white correction liquid used to blot out mistakes).

At this time, I had responsibility for preparing operational duties for officers at two police stations, as well as mutual aid for the woman's peace movement at Greenham Common and the miners' strike up north. It was hard enough covering busy periods due to sporting events, staff sickness and rest days without the added pressure of the other two. Just as I finished duties, there would be a call for ten officers to cover some music festival. By then I'd pulled my hair out. Apart from using the Tippex to change the duty sheet, I was at risk of sniffing the stuff to stop me going mad!

Thursday evenings were busy, and I'd arrive home with a bundle of court files to study for the following morning. As station sergeant, it was my duty to prosecute at the magistrate's court, where I had to pit my wits against defence solicitors. The files ranged from motoring offences to public order and minor crimes. You had to be prepared for the offender pleading not guilty, and the evidence needed to be convincing and not merely hearsay or suggestive. Then there was the cross examination, and hopefully a guilty verdict. Admittedly, four hours of overtime to read the files helped.

The miners' strike was a difficult situation and, due to my knee problems, I wasn't in the best physical state to face the harsh reality of bruising battles with a hardy bunch of people protecting their jobs down the coal mines. I had a lot of sympathy for them as they were only trying to obtain better pay and conditions.

My superintendent was a man who didn't suffer fools gladly and I got on really well with him. Some days he would come down and take me out for lunch to break the monotony from my desk duties. He was also the public order training officer for the force and carried a lot of clout.

One day, I asked him outright what he thought about the idea of me joining the others to go north on strike duty. He shook his head and said, 'you are not even trained in public order, plus the gammy leg – no chance'. The following day, he called me to his office and told me to stay on after my normal hours. I wasn't sure of the reason why, until he came in dressed in full riot gear. He handed me some protection gear and I followed him to the backyard. Two hours later, exhausted after the private tuition, I was now ready for action. He advised me not to lead from the front if things got out of hand as his job was on the line if I got injured.

Much has been written about the miners' strike and about the rights and wrongs of the police involvement in it. My own opinion is that we were used as a political tool to deal with actual and potential incidents of public disorder and, to this extent, often found ourselves up against it. I have never in my life seen so many police vans in convoy along the motorways of England. There were literally hundreds from every corner of the country.

On arrival we were billeted in Grimsby in large compounds. The facilities were excellent, but the hours were long and arduous – starting

About to experience life down a coal mine (me standing, 4th from right). Standing centre at the back was one of the tallest officers in the police force, who worked with me in Oxford

out on our journey at 2am in the morning and arriving in either Nottingham or Sheffield at 4am ready for the day. I saw action when the 'flying' pickets would suddenly descend on a coal pit and create an ugly confrontation on the picket line. Insults were traded and jostling was a regular occurrence. Contrary to stories circulating in the press at the time, relations between the police and miners, with a few highly publicised exceptions, were very good.

I spent several weeks in Sheffield and Nottingham, and even went down a coal mine myself, which in many ways shocked me. The journey down the lift shaft must have taken twenty minutes, which left me in no doubt we were miles underground. Then, the noise of rumbling coal and black dust everywhere. I then experienced first-hand walking along an uneven surface to the coal face with a light on my head, dirty water dripping all over my face, and at the same time trying not to smash my head against the planks holding up whatever was above me. It was sheer hell and one of the scariest experiences of my life. I couldn't get out quickly enough. I remember having many a long conversation with striking miners about the hardship they endured and why any man would want to send their sons underground in such awful conditions. I suppose this was the only work available.

To the relief of my superintendent, I managed to avoid injury.

BACK TO COWLEY

After the best part of four years at Didcot, I was transferred back to Cowley as detective sergeant, a job I relished. I was in the real world again, away from rural disputes, fishing rights, coursing, court work and parochial fall-outs.

I was lucky as this was an energetic station with an excellent detective inspector, who gave the sergeants freedom to do their own thing. Some of the old workhorses were still there moaning about

At my desk as a detective sergeant at Cowley Police Station

the lack of overtime, whilst a new breed of university detectives with 'mickey mouse' degrees were lording it above others. Nonetheless, I had a decent squad and spent a very enjoyable ten years there building up a good rapport with colleagues and the public alike.

During this time, the force introduced new guidelines, following the much publicised miscarriage of justice scandals. No detectives were allowed to stay on the CID after seven years as the authorities believed you were either corrupt or getting too close to criminals. I believe the force completely miscalculated this situation as they moved experienced detectives back to uniform where they served out the rest of their career as uniform carriers, just waiting for their pensions. It's easy to replace people, but not investigation skills, expertise and experience. With all this experience gone, and morale at an all-time low, the force suffered greatly in the fight against crime. It didn't help that some were allowed to continue their detective duties, causing others bitter resentment. I was one of the few who survived, with the boss telling me, 'you can't teach an old dog new tricks. We'll leave you alone.'

It was at this point in my career that I put my experience and learning about serious crime into action. As detective sergeant, and more than often acting detective inspector for long periods, I had to take on the more serious crimes, like complex fraud, suspicious deaths, robberies, public order offences with multiple offenders and crimes that received notoriety through the press. I was also involved in protracted murder investigations in other regions of the force, which took me away for long periods of time. In doing so I saw so much profound pain, suffering and dysfunction that these events would be permanently etched in my memory. Thankfully the names and crimes have become blurred over the passing years.

For all the long hours and complex cases, I always really enjoyed the process of police detective work, which required a great deal of patience and perseverance together with close team work to get the right results.

I was always fascinated by the recovery of fingerprints from a crime scene, a process which has been vital for forensic science for well over a hundred years. As we know, human fingerprints are unique to each individual and never change during your lifetime. This is why many criminals consider the use of gloves essential in the act of committing crime. During my detective days, once a person was charged with a certain crime, their fingerprints were taken by pressing their fingers onto an ink block and then transferred to a special pad for comparison with those left at a crime scene. Once the match was made the evidence was rarely challenged, and in most cases guilty pleas were entered at court. This was fine provided the police had a suspect's fingerprints in the first case.

Sir Alec Jeffreys revolutionised crime fighting in 1984 at his laboratory in Leicester when he discovered DNA fingerprints, which meant that the tiniest speck of body tissue or fluid could be used to link a suspect to any crime. From then on no killer could sleep soundly at night and hundreds of murders, some going back fifty years, have since been solved using this method. My own dealings with this new technology ranged from proving serious sexual offences to woundings and attempted murders. The tiniest fragment of clothing, fluid and hair tissues were taken from the victim and analysed at the forensic laboratory against samples taken from the suspect.

Around about 1987, I was advised to push for promotion to inspector, which didn't appeal to me at the time. I was earning good money, with no real shift work. Inspectors had a built-in allowance, didn't get overtime and worked long hours on shifts. The possibility of another house move, and the children's education to a less desirable area, was also quite daunting. Nevertheless, I gave in to the pressure from my bosses. Again, like the promotion exams, a lot of preparation was required to have any chance.

I prepared for the board by doing some research, but certainly not enough. The other four candidates were graduates and there was no guarantee any of us would pass. I was nervous and didn't want to let myself down on the day. The formal interview arrived and a panel of senior officers asked many difficult questions over the course of about

45 minutes. At the end of the interview, I got up from my chair pleased that it was over without any major mishaps. Then, it happened: as I made my way to the exit I was confronted by three doors; all of which were the same size and colour. Now, which of them was the exit? I tried the one in the middle only to find myself stumbling into the cupboard with its sprung hinges. How embarrassing! Out I come dishevelled and confused to see smiles on their faces. They then proceeded to point out the right door where I made a sharp exit. Now, you might be thinking that, in accordance with all good interview protocols, such an incident would be confined to just those present during the event. Not at all ... By the time I'd got back to the station, the chief superintendent was waiting for me with tears of laughter running down his face. The sods had phoned him to relay the story!

I failed the board. Naturally, I never wanted it in the first place! That was it, I left it alone and never tried again, which, in some ways, was a blessing in disguise. I had seen the effect it had on others, who became bitter and twisted on failing them.

This led to me drowning my sorrows with a game of cards at a pub in Oxford. The card school of about twelve of us continued late into the night when someone shouted 'police are here'. The landlord was fond of the booze and wasn't in the habit of locking the doors; in fact, this night they weren't even closed. Amazingly enough, this particular night everybody had finished drinking and were in the throes of leaving. I decided to make a quick exit to avoid being caught out and scrambled through the toilet window into the garden and over a six-foot-high fence.

Then disaster struck when my trousers got caught on the railing leaving me dangling with one leg either side of the fence. Looking up at me were two young policewomen who didn't know me from Adam. I heard them shout, 'we have one'. With a little help they freed me from a rather painful experience. Then the moment of truth, when the sergeant arrived on the scene, took one look at me, shook his head in disbelief, uttering expletives as he walked off. Not my finest hour.

THE HUNGERFORD MASSACRE

The Hungerford massacre in August 1987 comes to mind as one the worst random killings in UK history. I was not due to go into work until the afternoon but got a call at lunchtime to immediately report to the police station. By now news was breaking via the radio and television of a serious shooting incident in Hungerford, some twenty miles south of Oxford. Together with a colleague, who incidentally came from Hungerford, we made our way to the town. All communications were cut off to and from Hungerford because of the number of 999 calls being made, so my colleague was unable to contact his parents to make sure they were safe. The Thames Valley Police firearms squad were training some forty miles away and the police helicopter was in for repair. Only two telephone lines were in operation at Hungerford police station. All in all, a disaster.

It took ages to get to Hungerford, despite being waved through by police officers on traffic duty. What awaited us was a battleground, with bodies strewn all over the place. The police chiefs were rushing around in panic and the shooter (Michael Ryan) was still on the loose somewhere in the town. This mass shooting was unprecedented and the police were not prepared for the onslaught. When we got to the incident control centre, panic had set in. One of our officers had been shot dead and was still in his police car. Fear was the order of the day. It was all so different then, as firearms were not issued to officers as a matter of routine. First you had to convince an Assistant Chief Constable of their need, then locate an authorised user, who drove to police headquarters, opened the safe and made his way to the scene.

The first task was to get background information on Ryan, and figure out where he was likely to be hiding out. By now he had killed his mother and set their house ablaze. To complicate matters, the streets were too dangerous to visit as Ryan was a sharpshooter armed with two automatic sniper's rifles and handguns. The irony of it all is that he practised his deadly skills a couple of miles away from my home.

Hundreds of police descended on the little market town, better known for its antique shops and restaurants, and the tabloid press was everywhere. When the police marksmen arrived they took up positions at every vantage point. Later that afternoon, Ryan was spotted entering a school and the building was surrounded by police. It was time to get out on the streets and see the carnage first hand. Sixteen people lay dead, with grief and despair everywhere. Meanwhile, a police sniper had Ryan in his sights as he stood by a window in the school. He was holding the weapons but not threatening anyone. Then a shot rang out – Ryan lay dead from his own bullet.

I suppose a sense of relief entered my mind. It was now time to get to work and find a firm motive for the killings. I spent a couple of weeks investigating one particular murder, a man in his forties out walking his dog. By chance he came across Ryan, who shot him dead on the footpath. This was the first time I dealt with the tabloid press and they destroyed their reputation in my eyes by behaving outrageously with families. One day, I was taking a witness statement from the daughter of the deceased when a man of the cloth knocked on the door. The family had been warned about the press and the depths they would go to get pictures and a story. I looked at the man, dressed as a vicar, and asked for some identification. It turned out he was a reporter from one of the tabloids. How low can a human being stoop to get a story?

No motive was ever found for why Michael Ryan killed so many innocent people in his own town, some of them his family and neighbours. Some good came out of the shootings, however, with new firearms laws introduced, and firearms routinely being carried in selected police vehicles. The police sniper, who had Ryan in his sights, was a man I served with in my early days. Now a sergeant in charge of the firearms unit, I saw him years later and asked him why he didn't shoot Ryan after all the misery and mayhem he caused. His reply was so typical of the man: 'I had him in my sights with the rifle cocked and ready to fire. He was standing by a window alone, with his guns resting on his shoulders. I was very well aware of his killings, but at this time, he wasn't threatening anybody. Had he lifted the guns and pointed them, I would have shot him.' What an honourable and decent man.

HOME LIFE AND FAMILY GET-TOGETHERS

At last, back to normality, when I managed to spend some quality time with Sally and the boys. Both boys were now at primary school, a stone's throw from our house. Duncan was now well on his way to becoming an accomplished musician and Stephen's first touch on the football field left a lot to be desired, causing me great anxiety, ranting, raving and frothing at the mouth. Two of the great loves in my life were music and sport, and I was so fortunate that Duncan had an interest in music and Stephen one for sport. We had a busy life, with Duncan's guitar and piano, and me travelling the country with Stephen. It was a wonderful time in our lives. Both lads gave us immense pleasure and never brought an ounce of trouble back home. We always had great fun with them and enjoyed their company and still do.

I always enjoyed having a guitar to strum about the house and loved country music. Sally and the boys would regularly be treated (or possibly subjected) to the same few numbers that I could remember the chords to. Numbers I enjoyed playing included 'Sorrow' by The Merseys and 'Okie From Muskogee' by Merle Haggard. Now, as I often struggled to remember the chords to many of the songs, my trick when playing to anyone for the first time was to play just a snippet and then make an excuse to put the guitar down. It seemed to work and the 'always leave them wanting more' quote never seemed so apt!

When Duncan started playing the guitar as an eight year old, I would drive him each Saturday morning to lessons with a chap who was able to turn his hand to any instrument. Duncan now jokes that all the beginner songs he first learnt on the guitar were actually requests from me. I would sit in a comfy armchair watching his lesson and request to hear my favourite songs. 'How does "Apache" go? Play that one.' Numbers by Cliff Richard and the Shadows featured heavily in Duncan's early repertoire.

Meanwhile, holidays with Sally and the boys were always fun. We spent some lovely summer breaks throughout their childhood in Devon, Cornwall, the Isle of Wight and South Wales. After the hustle and bustle of police life it was a nice time to relax, play board games, kick a ball around on the beach and savour an ice cream or two. Sally always laughed when I would dive around saving penalties from the boys as if my life depended on it. The competitive streak never wavered, despite the wavering knee joints!

Keeping in touch with the Irish side of the family was important; therefore, I was delighted when, after a gap of eleven years, my mother and Granny Kate were able to stay with us in Oxford one summer. I'm sure much of Nancy's suitcase was taken up with a pile of *Sligo Champion* newspapers as well as half a dozen bottles of my favourite

Michael with his first grandchildren, Duncan and Stephen (1984)

Chef Sauce (an Irish brown sauce which you couldn't buy in England at the time).

We returned to visit Cliffoney quite a few times too, especially in the mid-eighties, when for a time we seriously considered selling up and making a home in the Emerald Isle. For various reasons this didn't happen; however, I was pleased that the boys got to spend more time with their grandparents, their great Granny Kate as well as the wider family. I remember watching the boys playing happily with the animals on the farm or kicking a ball with a neighbour's boy across the road. Seeing them enjoy the experience was a lovely sight and reminded me of how I had felt as a child. I also remember the last day of one trip to Cliffoney, when Duncan broke his foot jumping from a haystack. As we were catching the ferry the next day, I had no option but to piggyback him up and down the ferry steps. We managed to get him home to tell the tale, but only just!

In the spring of 1985 we took the boys and Sally's parents over to stay with my brother Pat and his wife Sheila. How we managed to complete the long journey with six of us and baggage crammed into one medium-sized car I will never know. It was the only occasion when both my parents and Sally's spent time together. Sally's dad was particularly fascinated by the bog and had a go at cutting the turf.

Sally's mum and dad visit Nancy and Michael

Everyone got on well and there were plenty of tears when we had to say goodbye (in a good way, I hasten to add!).

Another very special and first meeting occurred in the summer of 1989 when I was holidaying in Cliffoney. By chance, an opportunity arose for my parents, my granny Kate and the siblings to all meet up together for the first time ever. Although it may sound strange, over the years, with a twenty year age gap between eldest and youngest sibling and several of us being in different locations, this had not been possible. Fortunately, my sister Mary happened to be staying in Cliffoney at the same time as me and this led to a telephone call to my brother Pete, who thankfully was able to travel across from his home in Roscrea, in the south of the country. The day itself was such a special event, with the sun shining and a family photo shoot taking place in the front garden, just in front of Nancy's beautifully arranged

We finally all got together in Cloonkeen: Pat, me, Michael, Pete, John and Thomas; Tina, Joan, Mary and Ann

flowerbeds of all colours. As well as being a day of fun and good humour, it was also a poignant occasion, as at the time my father's health was in decline. When I think back now, I am delighted that he got the chance to see all of his children together in Cloonkeen.

On another visit to Cliffoney, I recall witnessing first-hand my brother Thomas's antics, which were legendary within the village. We had been to the pub and, after a good night's drinking, Thomas and I staggered gingerly back to the farmhouse into the kitchen, making sure Nancy didn't hear us. Anyway, we were both hungry and the bold Thomas raided the fridge to find sausages, bacon, eggs, the lot. However, the gas wouldn't light, so off he goes in the dark to find the gas bottle which Nancy had hidden away from him in the hayshed. (Nancy was frightened Thomas would set the house ablaze.) After an eternity and a lot of noise, Thomas stumbled in and lit the gas. The next challenge was to prevent the crackling from the frying pan from disturbing the mother. No better man than Thomas to place Nancy's best clean bed linen over the pan to stop the hissing noise from the cooking. I thought at the time what about the washing up. In a flash Thomas had put everything away in the cupboard, greasy plates and

Nancy with me, Duncan and Stephen (1991)

all, nothing washed. Needless to say, we stayed out of Nancy's way in the morning!

ANIMALS AND DIY ANTICS

I have reminisced about my boys enjoying playing with animals on the farm in Cloonkeen; however, I should also say that they were not exactly in short supply of animals back in their own home in Oxford. In fact, by the time of the late-eighties the farm life I had enjoyed as a child seemed to have come full circle and been miraculously transported to my Oxford home.

In addition to the henhouse holding two dozen chickens, we now had an aviary of canaries, a caged blue budgerigar (very common then but seldom seen these days), a dozen fish in the pond, a rabbit, a cat and a lively boxer dog. One of the difficulties with this set up was that the cat and dog didn't get along. There were times when I would look out of the kitchen window and stare forlornly to witness animal carnage. Mud and stones would be flying through the air as our excited dog sprinted a hundred miles an hour, full pelt towards the chicken coop chasing after the terrified cat. The bottom of the garden, where the two dozen chickens were kept, looked and smelt like a farmyard. Looking back, I guess I must have been keen to have pets at the time; these days the idea of that number of animals fills me with dread. Having said that, they were fun times and I still enjoy looking after my aviary of birds to this day, an idea originally inspired by my good friend and best man, Allan Sheppard. Thanks, Allan!

Whilst not dealing with unruly animals, Sally and I were encountering all sorts of DIY mishaps, which I'm sure Sally won't mind me recounting. One incident occurred when we were decorating our spare room. Sally was certainly a daddy's girl and always listened to his advice above mine! Anyway, I was in the middle of wallpapering our spare bedroom, and instead of cutting one strip of paper at a time, Sally had the great idea of cutting the whole roll – 'My dad always does that', she proclaimed. In she comes to take over the cutting, which would have been fine except that every length ended up about a foot short. Needless to say, she was banished from the decorating for some time after that incident.

On another occasion we had a large greenhouse in the garden when we moved to our current house. It took up too much room and, although I didn't want to get rid of it, I was keen to reduce it in size. If I do say so myself, I did a great job of dismantling the sections and putting them together again. I was very pleased with the result and called Sally to show her. Ever helpful, she decided to put the wheelbarrow in it. In she marches, completely forgetting that protruding from the front of the barrow was a big metal bar, and crash, straight through the back it goes, smashing all the glass. I don't know how I did it, but I kept my cool.

Meanwhile, despite ongoing knee and back problems, I wasn't put off playing sport, especially football. The one major obstacle I now had to overcome, however, was the ticking of an older clock. You see, I was now heading towards the early side of forty and playing against fellas

CID soccer team (front row, far right)

some twenty years my junior. Add into the mix a competitive streak and you had a perfect storm.

Throughout the 1980s, I made more footballing comebacks than George Best, and should have packed in years earlier as my knees had more or less gone. Despite this, I couldn't resist the temptation when teams were short of players to tie up the boots and relive the old times. Near the end of the decade I had my last game for Oxford, against a team from London. I was told to man-mark this particular player who very seldom handled the ball, which is most unusual in Gaelic football. He flicked the ball past me with deft touches every time, making me look the complete eejit. Enough was enough, and next time, whack, down he goes (I flattened him), red card and the line again for Henry. I thought nothing more of it until after the game when I was told the player was an Irish international soccer player. Gerry Armstrong (for it was he) had scored the winning goal for Ireland against hosts Spain in the 1982 World Cup finals. He'd come along as a spectator and got roped into playing. Oops!

I'm afraid to say my days of red mist as a player also carried through into my days as a spectator. By the early 1990s Stephen's football ability was taking shape. He was now captaining the county and had trials for the England under-14 squad. I have to say, I had great expectations of him being a professional, with Sally and me living the 'high life' from his earnings. He actually got to a good standard playing for youth teams at Peterborough, Swindon and Oxford United. Anyway, on one occasion he was playing for Oxford and an up-and-coming youth coach at the time, called McClaren, decided to substitute my lad early in the game. Never being one to hold back my feelings, I promptly marched up to the coach and told him what I thought about his decision. 'You're going nowhere McClaren as long as you have a hole in your a***!' I bellowed, and marched off thinking that was the last I'd see of him.

Unfortunately, that statement has come back to bite me many times as this chap destined to go nowhere was actually Steve McClaren, who went on to have great success as coach for Man United, when they won

Karen, Duncan, Stephen and Alison in 1995

the Champions league and treble in 1999, and, more humiliatingly for me, went on to be head coach of the English national team in 2007. My lads still tease me about this story to this day. All I can say is that thank God Steve McClaren didn't guide England to win the World Cup!

At a family wedding: Stephen, Alison, me, Sally, Sally's mum,
Karen and Duncan

During the nineties two girls entered the scene who would be a loving part of our family from that point on. In 1992 Duncan met Karen and three years later Stephen met Alison. Up until that point, no girlfriends had ventured near the door as the lads were well aware of the grilling that lay in store for them. Duncan reminds me that when Karen, who is a brunette, first arrived to meet us, my teasing quip was 'What happened to the blonde one?'

Karen and Duncan met at school and both shared a love of music. When they were students they enjoyed earning a few more pennies by busking in Oxford. The covered market in Oxford (where I had policed a few years previously) was a popular spot, due to the acoustics, and I recall them returning home one afternoon with a bucket full of coins, plus a few chops from the butcher opposite them. I always thought the steaks were too high!

Stephen also met Alison at school and they were both keen runners. Alison was a young shy lass when she first entered the fray, being only sixteen at the time, and would run to our house to meet Stephen. She quickly ran away too when she started hearing my jokes! I am afraid to say that with the passing of time Alison has lost the shyness and now gives as good as she gets.

Chapter Eight

A DIFFERENT BEAT

PRESS OFFICER

After ten years at Cowley it was now the mid-nineties and I needed a fresh challenge. The chief of police considered it too risky for me to resume operational duties due to my numerous knee operations. Consequently, I was offered a daytime job as scrutineer for the area – a big word describing my work at playing with the crime figures. You see, each police area had a monthly crime target, and no area wanted an increase in serious crimes like robberies and burglaries as it affected the public's confidence in the police and, more importantly for some senior officers, the chances of further promotion. The job involved setting up a new crime unit in Oxford, handling reports of crime from the public and deciding how to progress them. I had to supervise five officers and three civilians.

I recall that one of the officers had a habit of walking into the city centre during his lunch break. This was fine until one day the superintendent rushed into my office demanding to know why one of my officers was patrolling the city centre, in full uniform, wearing cream carpet slippers! The officer liked to make himself comfortable in the office by removing his shoes and replacing them with something a little less formal. On returning to the station, he wondered what all the fuss was about – until I pointed to his feet!

It was also at this time that I started handling calls from the press, which soon led to a new chapter in my life which I could never have foreseen. Alongside my work as scrutineer, I was appointed press officer, which involved me liaising with the media, and acting as the 'face' and 'voice' of the police via both local and national media outlets, including radio, newspapers and television.

Many of the cases I had to discuss with the media related to serious crimes like rape, wounding and murder, so were sensitive. I had the trust of senior police officers and wasn't going to let them down with loose talk, especially to people I didn't really know.

Because of my role, journalists in television, radio and print would be keen to 'chat' to get a heads-up or exclusive on the latest news stories – I wasn't daft or stupid enough to think it was for my good looks or sense of humour. I had some bad experiences with the 'red top' national newspapers at the Hungerford killings, and saw first-hand the lengths they would go to get stories. The local press, however, had a good reputation with the police and did not want to tarnish their image by misquoting an officer. Trust on both sides was the key, although I was well aware that a good juicy story could be sold on for thousands of pounds by some rogue journalist.

In my role as press officer – promoting a knife amnesty

After numerous courses on public relations and the Official Secrets Act, I was let loose to be my own man and given plenty of scope to speak to the press. On my first radio interview I was very nervous, and used far too many ifs and buts. The more I did, however, the more confident and fluent I became.

I found television equally daunting at first and was faced with different problems; for example, when a camera crew took exception to me wearing a check coloured jacket as it twinkled in front of camera lights and did not make for good viewing. On radio you can go into a studio unshaven in your underpants and nobody would be any the wiser. On television you have to look your best.

The live television broadcasts were particularly testing because I had no idea what I was going to be asked. If a news story was suddenly to break, I could be asked to comment with little or no preparation. I was nervous and always handled them with caution. Not surprisingly, the recorded interviews were usually better as I could repeat the interview and mistakes could be edited out. Talking of editing, for television interviews my face was invariably edited – in the form of make-up artists applying powder in the studio to reduce the light on my face. If not careful I'd end up looking like I'd been lying on a sunny beach without sun cream for two weeks!

It's amazing to think back now about the number of times national television took an interest in relatively minor crime. I remember one particular occasion when a local chap, who was in charge of allotments in south Oxford, contacted me about several break-ins to their sheds. Garden tools were being stolen and the break-ins were causing a lot of damage; in response, the allotment owners had taken to staying at the allotment overnight to protect their belongings. The *Oxford Mail* initially ran the story and, before I knew it, the nationals had it, with the BBC running it on their main news bulletins. Amazing really. I recall my uncle Kevin mentioning that he watched me being interviewed from his armchair in Cliffoney.

On another occasion I reported on a story about Metro cars being stolen regularly from Park & Ride car parks in Oxford. The BBC

With the fictional detective (Morse): me with a colleague and actors
John Thaw and Kevin Whately

re-enacted a theft, but needed a youth to be filmed doing the break in. My youngest, Stephen, had the dubious honour of breaking into the car and running away from the scene, which he carried out to perfection. Worryingly so, you might say!

While Stephen was trying to damage Metro doors, Duncan was trying his hardest not to damage our family Metro. At this time I took personal responsibility for overseeing Duncan's first ever driving experience; something I recall very well, but for the wrong reasons. Rather naively, I decided that the best way for him to learn was to throw him in at the deep end. Anyway, we drove off to the end of the road and prepared to turn right. Indicators on, look left, look right. Great. At this stage, things were going well. Then we started to head towards a notoriously sharp bend, which I had failed to recognise as downright dangerous for a novice driver. On approach the car started to veer off towards the curb and a ten foot wall. To avoid disaster I was forced to grab the only instrument within arm's length and perform a handbrake turn whilst grabbing the steering wheel. Poor Duncan had the shakes, but we eventually managed to get round the bend and home in one piece. Thereafter, I became a back seat driver and left the driving instructing to the professionals! I think Sally was driven around the bend (pardon the pun) too but from the stress of the boys' first outings in a car!

During my time as press officer, I also managed to meet a few celebrities. Oxford is famous for many things: the 'dreaming spires' of its universities, the ancient artefacts of the Ashmolean museum, Sir Roger Banister and his first sub-four-minute mile, and of course its famous detective. Before you ask, no, that's not me! The BBC television police programme *Inspector Morse* was compulsive viewing in the early to mid-1990s and was filmed in and around Oxford. The main character, played by actor John Thaw, would occasionally pop in to see us to check up facts of how the real detectives would deal with murders and serious crime. He was a lovely man, who was quiet and easy to get on with. Believe it or not, I was offered a cameo part in the series before I retired, but never got round to taking it up. What I didn't know at the time was my dearly departed sister Tina was a huge fan and had every episode, with the books to match.

While press officer I appeared on various local and national news programmes, including *Sky News*, Radio 4's *Today* and *News at Ten*, as well as some more light-hearted shows, such as ITV's *GMTV*. All in all, it was an interesting role and one I enjoyed.

RETIREMENT REFLECTIONS

The force had been good to me and, after several enjoyable years working at Kidlington and with the press, I retired in February 1998 after over thirty years' service. Although I never appeared before another promotion board, I was made temporary inspector before retiring.

As for the police of today, although I understand that things have and need to change, I do have some misgivings regarding the direction things have gone. A system that favours the criminal, political correctness gone mad, too much focus on personal gain, objectives not aligned with fighting real crime, and a lack of real bobbies on the beat all continue to frustrate me.

Decommissioning local police stations has in my opinion been a complete disaster and was an idiotic idea. They were always the necessary symbol of law and order in the community. In my day, it was not uncommon for stranded motorists to call at the police station (every little town had one) in the middle of the night to seek directions to the nearest 24-hour petrol station. Now compare those situations with the present day, when motorists have to call on a 24-hour petrol station to seek the whereabouts of the nearest open police station.

Another thing that I feel has changed drastically since my time is the way police officers are dressed. In my years in uniform, you always had to be smartly turned out, which immediately gave you confidence and respect in dealing with the good, the bad and the ugly. For the most part, today we see police officers without any form of headgear, denim-style trousers which have never seen an iron, boots that have never been polished and open neck shirts. Whatever happened to the pre-duty parade, when you had to look your best in front of the sergeant? Gone are the days when the public would recognise a policeman by his smart uniform. I understand the counter argument about the older traditional uniform being impractical and inflexible; however, my feeling is that it presented a more professional and visible image to the public, which in turn gained respect. Of course, police officers reflect the society they come from, and nowadays are armed to the teeth with all sorts of gadgets, sprays and weapons. Thankfully, in my early days I was only armed with a small baton, handcuffs, whistle, radio (which sometimes worked) and common sense. Bringing back the smart 'bobby' on the beat and rebuilding trust between communities and officers would, I feel, reduce the fear of crime, ensure continuity, and increase visibility and faith in the once proud police force.

Oxford City Police hold a reunion a couple of times a year, when we meet up and discuss various topics relating to our time in the force. The recruiting inspector at the time of my interview told me a story recently of how lucky I was to get into the police at the time.

Not only were there a lot of applicants for the one position on offer, the Chief Constable was a man of great character and deliberated in great detail prior to making any decision. He did the final vetting of the applicants himself and short-listed four for final interview. I was one of them.

The inspector was honest enough to say that the other applicants were better educated and, in his opinion, well ahead of me in experiences of life. To compound my problem, I failed to turn up on the given day, which I have to say I don't recall. The chief asked for the final selection to be deferred until I arrived. The rest is history.

I never had the chance to speak to the Chief Constable again as, sadly, he died a couple of years after he interviewed me. I'd have loved to thank him for the confidence he'd shown in me and for making a decision which ultimately changed the course of my life. I would like to think that he wasn't disappointed. May he rest in peace.

BACK TO WORK

Although retired from the job, I was too young to stay at home and drive Sally mad, so I ended up working for the police again over the next few years as a civilian in various offices.

First port of call was a crime call centre at Witney police station. The detective inspector knew me from my days in Oxford. The job sounded interesting, but why did an ex-inspector leave the role early? I was soon to find out.

In the office were six friendly girls in their twenties and thirties, who answered calls from the general public and then completed the necessary paperwork. The first week was fine, with no problems. By then I had settled in and, despite not liking it, turned a blind eye to the radio playing in the office. With each passing day the radio got louder, until I blew my top and took it away from them. Now the trouble started. No smiles to greet Henry in the morning, no coffee, no friendly banter, in fact all but one refused to speak to me.

Tea breaks were like night clubs, with the CID boys hanging round the girls like bees around a honey pot. Now I upset them as well by ordering them out unless it was work-related. I was now firmly the bad boy, and things were set to get worse.

One morning all the girls ran out of the office crying – I had got on to one of them and they all rallied round and ran to the toilet en masse. The boss heard the commotion and came in smiling. He was absolutely delighted that I had got them organised at last. After I calmed them down with some sweet talking and doughnuts we all got on like a house on fire.

One lunchtime I came back to the office with two canaries that I had bought. I left them on the desk and went off to a meeting. When I came back in there was great activity, with my two feathery birds being chased around in the office by non-feathery birds who were desperately trying to catch them.

I watched on, greatly amused, as they climbed tables in their high heels before eventually catching them. I spent four years in the post and was sorry to leave.

Whilst working at Abingdon police station another incident occurred, which for once backfired on me. The detective sergeant at the station was very witty and a bit of a wind-up merchant. In particular, he liked to tease me by talking brashly and imitating the late northern Irish politician Dr Ian Paisley, with his thunderous rhetoric and bull-like voice. You could hear him a mile away. I suffered a lot of mickey taking from him, and waited my chance for retribution. It came one hot summer's day, when he asked me to accompany him to a nearby garden centre in his search for a new shed. Once in the confined space of the car, he was in my ear hole the whole journey with his impressions and, by the time we arrived, I had had not just an earful but a bellyful. Anyway, after browsing around the garden centre for a little while, he took an interest in a large shed. At this moment I smiled, as I knew I had him. Once he was inside, I locked the door and cleared off with the key. With the shed located well away from other customers and staff, and his police radio and mobile phone in the car, unfortunately for him he was unable to contact anybody. It was initially my intention to just leave him in for half an hour or so to teach him a lesson; however, I got distracted and returned to the police station having forgotten all about him! It was only later in the day, when I heard that police had been contacted to deal with one of their men locked in a shed and suffering from heat exhaustion, that I remembered him! I was a worried man and was so relieved that he didn't suffer any lasting health issues. Thankfully he forgave me and we remain good friends.

New pastures ahead, when in the early 2000s I took on the role of coroner's officer for Oxfordshire. Part of a team of three, the others had medical knowledge prior to joining but this work was completely new to me and I had to learn the ropes fairly quickly. You received reports of death, made enquiries on behalf on the coroner, and liaised with relatives. I had to investigate causes of death, obtain written statements and assemble evidence from police officers, medics and other authorities to prepare a file for the coroner. Identification of the deceased was often difficult, especially if a person died tragically in an accident.

You had to sort out and attend post-mortems, ensuring bodies were released to the relatives as quickly as possible, as well as arranging for the relevant people to attend inquests. All in all, quite a depressing job. You also had to write up reports using the correct medical terms from pathologists, consultants, GPs, and legal representatives. Once a month you were on call outside your normal working day, and had to attend major incidents like murders, multiple fatalities and suspicious deaths.

Due to the area we covered, we had to receive soldiers from the wars in the Middle East. A time of reflection on the futility of all conflicts. Dealing with the bodies was difficult, but even worse was having to deal with the bereaved families, who often had to wait for years to have the inquests into their loved ones' death heard.

Nevertheless, all in all, the coroner's officer job was an absorbing one offering a vital public service.

A NEW RADIO CAREER

The radio, or wireless as it was always known, conjures up special memories for me of growing up in Cliffoney during the fifties and sixties. The invention of the transistor radio – which could be hidden under the bedclothes and well away from your parent's ears – added to the revolution that was taking place. Down the decades, that humble box has kept me updated on news events; introduced me to singers and music; and provided wonderful commentaries of many great sporting events, including, of course, those hugely memorable Gaelic football matches. There was no great mystery about the radio, in that it was a world of faceless people who entered our homes at all times of day and night and, in doing so, became the best of friends over the years. Ironically it allowed me to imagine far better pictures than television now provides.

I never for a minute imagined I would become one of those faceless people, lucky enough to experience life as a broadcaster with the BBC. I believed all radio presenters were qualified journalists

Starting out as a BBC broadcaster in 1995

with backgrounds in media studies. Here I was, a copper with little education, big feet and a big mouth, who was fortunate enough to be blessed with the gift of the gab. Timing and location are always factors in a person's fortunes, and for me they couldn't have been better.

At the time I was coming towards the end of my police career, and to be quite honest did not have a clue what awaited me. Security work – often a path for those leaving the police – did not interest me one iota.

Anyway, one day, whilst being interviewed at BBC Radio Oxford on police duties, I happened to bump into the boss and mentioned the fact that another radio station was in the throes of broadcasting an Irish programme. It was just a throwaway remark on my part. His response was negative, saying 'what about the Welsh and Scots?' I got the message.

In fact, he had a point, and you may ask, 'why an Irish radio programme and how did it come about?' Well, when I think back now, I suppose my reasons for promoting an Irish radio show were linked to both my frustration with the shortage of specialist radio programmes and my own experiences over the years as a radio listener struggling to get a decent broadcast for Irish news and music back home. For decades, listeners in the UK seeking out Irish radio coverage, many of whom were elderly Irish immigrants, had relied on Irish national radio as their only link with home. The reception difficulties with other stations made this hard to listen to, despite many empty promises made over the years by Irish government ministers about improving the quality, invariably at election times. I understood the value of an indigenous Irish radio station to the lives of the elderly Irish community in Britain, and this was uppermost on my mind when I saw an opportunity to maybe bring a little bit of the Emerald Isle into people's homes.

The deputy boss of Radio Oxford at the time, a decent man, obviously heard about my interest and asked me to do a demo tape. He liked my voice – at the time, local BBC was going through a transitional period, when Irish and Scottish voices were sometimes preferred to the traditional 'posh' English ones – and gave me the opportunity to be a guest, once a week for an hour, on the Bill Rennells evening radio show. Bill had just come from national Radio Two and I'm pleased to say, now well into his eighties, is still presenting and as popular as ever.

Things developed from there and the programme initially became *Irish Hour*, advertised as a mixture of chat and Irish music for the Irish community in Oxfordshire. I well remember it took a long time to gain the confidence to do a programme on my own. The first thing I had to master was how to operate the equipment in the studio and, I can tell you, it required a steep learning curve. For someone not familiar with its workings, the nearest I would describe it is that of a cockpit of an aeroplane. After much practice I got there in the end, but not before many long silent pauses. Sometimes I would forget

'Cheers!'

to open the microphone, or worse still, inadvertently say something not quite right when the microphone was open. The equipment has changed from reel-to-reel tape recording to high tech so many times over the years it has been difficult to keep on top of it.

Fortunately I had, over the years, gained some related experience as a mobile disc jockey, almost exclusively for Irish gigs. That was invaluable because it provided me with a visible audience reaction to playing certain songs and I could use that experience to assess how well the same track would be received by a radio audience.

Meanwhile, over on BBC Berkshire a new programme called *Irish Eye* was being aired. *Irish Eye* was the brainchild of Anne Morris and Kieran McGeary, who started off with a four hour radio show in 1995. A short while later some local radio stations merged across the south, creating BBC Thames Valley FM. In 1996 *Irish Hour* was subsumed into *Irish Eye* and Kieran initially led the programme, with Anne and me helping on the phones. When Kieran left to return to Waterford a couple of years later, where he now heads up the largest regional station in Ireland, it left me to take over the mic, where I have been ever since.

The programme, which provides a weekly infusion of music, culture and chat, is aired every Sunday afternoon and has become hugely popular across the south of England via traditional radio and, in more recent years, worldwide via the internet. Now with a large broadcasting sphere, the show has many regular listeners who email us from Canada, Mexico, Australia, New Zealand and America, some getting up at all hours, and most of them not even Irish. Two of the chaps I used to work with in Maye's Motors in Sligo listen to me online, one in Berwick, Australia and the other in Roscommon, Ireland. Actually, it's incredible how loyal listeners can be; I know that in the past one English couple made a regular Sunday trip from their home to the top of a hillside miles away to receive the programme.

Others join us from unlikely locations. Over the years convicts from prisons have written to us requesting special pieces of music. I recall that one such prisoner tried in vain to describe a Johnny Cash song by likening the title of the song to the words used by a witness in describing his appearance to the police when robbing a bank!

With regards to my style of broadcasting, I would describe myself as utterly laid back, perhaps too much so at times. My interviewing style is to listen to the person talking – not interrupting – and not like some disc jockeys, who seem to just love the sound of their own voice. I try to gently probe, but to be totally in control of the on-air discussion. I will never allow a guest who enters the studio, intent on plugging something for private gain, to dictate the conversation.

When I first started out on the radio, I received some invaluable advice from the late Sir Terry Wogan, who lived in our area and had heard the programme. He advised me to put a photo of a friend on the wall of the studio and imagine I was talking to that person when on air. Sir Terry also explained that it doesn't matter if you have one listener or a million – don't put on any airs and graces, and just be yourself. He thought that being Irish was a blessing as if we made mistakes they would usually be interpreted as us trying to be funny and that way we would get away with it!

Stand-ins for me over the years have included Graham Clifford, who at the time was the sports editor at the *Irish Post* newspaper in the UK. He returned to Ireland in later years and is now a feature writer and journalist with the daily *Irish Independent*. Current stand-in is ex-RTE producer and presenter, Al Ryan. When not available, I have sometimes had to record a three hour programme maybe a month before the programme was to be broadcast (often during some unearthly hour due to no studio being available). I have learnt some valuable lessons from this; for example, to avoid playing songs centred around tragic words such as 'fire' (as in Johnny Cash's 'Ring of Fire') or 'plane' (as in 'Silver Wings' by Merle Haggard) in case I inadvertently dropped a faux pas by playing what could be perceived as insensitive music immediately after a tragic event which there would have been know way of me foreseeing.

I have to say that I've had my moments with pre-recording

programmes. One such occasion some years back springs to mind when, after recording a three-hour special, I mistakenly hit the delete button instead of 'save'; in an instant I lost the entire programme! Another time, armed with a state-of-the-art digital recorder, I did three different interviews, only to discover I forgot to press the record button! I learnt a hard lesson.

The radio gives me an insight into other people's lives, maybe a little too much at times. I remember receiving some saucy letters from a woman in London, looking for a photograph of yours truly. For a bit of fun, I got hold of a picture of a workmate of mine from the police and sent it to her. Since that day I have never heard a word from her. Afterwards, I had some sleepless nights, thinking what about if the woman came to Oxford and recognised my mate out walking with his wife and kids!

Over the years, Sally always stepped in to answer the phones when Anne was on holiday, so when Anne retired in 2012 she was, with some reluctance, persuaded to join me permanently. Sally, like Anne, has a tremendous rapport with listeners, who look upon her as their special friend. She beats a regular path from the telephone area to the studio to do her share of the broadcasting. Sally's knowledge of country and Irish music is very good, and the programme has blossomed into a semi-chat show with celebrity interviews.

IRISH EYE INTERVIEWS

During my time with *Irish Eye*, I've been fortunate to interview many big names in Irish life, from actors, sports stars, and singers to government ministers. As you might expect, politicians are the most difficult to get straight answers from. Their skill in avoiding answers to a given question, or leading you down a different route altogether, can be both annoying and frustrating.

Robin Gibb of the super group the Bee Gees, together with his wife, Dwina, have popped into the studio several times to see me.

Meeting Paddy Reilly and the Dubliners, who I interviewed
many times, in Oxford

They lived in Oxfordshire and Dwina hails from Omagh, Co. Tyrone. They surprised me by telling me that Mullaghmore was one of their favourite holiday resorts, which they often visited without being recognised.

While chatting to Robin he relayed a story to me which could only happen in Ireland. According to Robin, Mick Jagger was visiting Mullingar in Ireland some years ago when a large group of star struck girls came running down the street towards him. Assuming that they were directing their attention at him, the Rolling Stones frontman started to groom himself in preparation for the usual hysteria he attracted. Next thing, to Jagger's surprise, the groupies completely ignored him and raced around the corner. Now, what an earth could have made these girls bypass one of the world's biggest stars? The arrival of Elvis? The Beatles? No – none other than country singer Big

With Robin Gibb of the Bee Gees in the studio

Tom[1], one of Ireland's biggest stars at the time, who was performing around the corner!

The story goes that, with his tail firmly between his legs, Mick Jagger entered the hall and asked Big Tom for his autograph. Apparently the big man duly obliged but failed to recognise who the autograph hunter was. An amazing story but not that surprising: the Irish are renowned for not putting famous people on a pedestal.

Val Doonican was probably the best person I have ever interviewed from the showbiz world. He was totally professional, sharp, witty, highly intelligent and actually listened to and responded to the questions directed at him. In contrast, some of the so-called stars of today can come across as boring, with huge egos, and only appear interested in themselves.

That's certainly not true of the famous singer Daniel O'Donnell, who is a real gentleman and once phoned me from the States to enquire about my health. He is the ultimate professional and people just love him. Many a time he has gone out of his way to visit me

---

[1] Ireland's 'King of Country Music', Big Tom McBride was the first artist to be inducted into the Irish Country Music Hall of Fame.

Stephen gets a 'Big Tom' T shirt for Christmas, much to
Duncan's amusement

in the studio, when other so-called big names would want money for
the privilege. There have been occasions when I interviewed him on
the telephone and came out to see lots of faces at the window as they
thought he was with me in the studio – and there's me thinking that
they were there to see me!

On the subject of Irish icons, I have always enjoyed having Foster
and Allen in the studio, with the squeeze box and guitar in tow. They
are two of the biggest names on the music circuit, with their easy
going sing-a-long style that has endeared them to millions of fans,
not just in Ireland but all over the world. The nicest fellows you would
wish to meet.

Ireland is famous for its 100,000 welcomes, 'cead mile failte', her
literary sons and daughters, her heroes and of course her love of music
and folklore. Although I have always loved country music, and it
would take centre stage for me, you may be surprised to learn that my
favourite song is Vic Damone's 'On The Street Where You Live' from

Me and Daniel O'Donnell in the BBC studio

the 1956 Broadway musical *My Fair Lady*. As for my own choice of favourite entertainer, from the Irish crop I would have to say that Johnny McEvoy, Mike Denver and Patsy Watchorn top the list. Other singers that I view in high regard include Elvis, Dean Martin and the great country singer, Waylon Jennings.

My claim to fame from a radio viewpoint is reuniting two world-class runners from the 1950s. Roger Bannister, the first sub-four-minute miler, was in the studio being interviewed by another presenter when I got speaking to him about Ireland's first Olympic champion, Ronnie Delaney, who won gold for Ireland in Melbourne in 1956. They had not met for over sixty years and I was delighted to be able to bring them together. I received a nice letter from them both thanking me.

Also through the medium of radio, I was able to reunite a long-lost brother and sister some years back. Sean Wilson, the famous Irish country singer, contacted me to see if I could possibly help to trace his uncle. His widowed mother living in Northern Ireland was as proud as punch of her son's success, but beneath her joy laid a deep sorrow concerning her long-lost brother, John, who went to England some

With Foster and Allen in the studio

fifty years previously and none of the family had seen or heard of him since. The only information they had was that he lived in the midlands area of England. Sean had just released his latest music album called *When Irish Eyes Are Smiling*, but little did he know that the title track would turn out to be prophetic. During my programme I asked for anyone listening who could help to trace John and, within a couple of days, John had been found and the family reunited. I was delighted to hear that brother and sister spent time together again, with Irish eyes smiling, before they died.

From the perspective of world news, I believe my interviews with the medical staff and survivors of the Omagh bombing (15 August, 1998), the day after the awful event, were the most harrowing moments for me. My studio interview with Steve Travers from The Miami Showband massacre in Northern Ireland (31 July, 1975) was also very emotional. I was in tears when he relayed the story of his horrific injuries and being left among the dead for ages. I believe the interview gave a powerful message of survival, forgiveness and hope for the future.

The Good Friday Agreement in Northern Ireland in 1998 was another historic occasion when my studio guests contributed to the debate. The peace agreement was such a long time arriving and involved so many false starts that people thought it would never happen.

Both Sally and I have a grip on the certainty that, for many of the listeners, the programme conjures up bittersweet feelings. There's laughter and tears, and sometimes both simultaneously. Certain songs bring that exquisite pain that memories so often evoke. Tunes like 'Absent Friends' and 'You're So Far Away' are amongst the most popular for that very reason.

Of course everyone can relate to the moment when a song or a piece of music not heard in decades comes on the radio. You are immediately transported to a different time and place that has special meaning for you. I always get emotional when I listen to Elvis Presley's music. The jet black hair and turned up lower lip are still there in my mind and conjure up visions of faces now long gone, which invokes a great sadness in me. His songs remind me of a time when the boys in the garage in Sligo would have the radio on blaring out Elvis in customer's cars they were supposed to be repairing. Now, most of those men, six in all, and roughly the same age as me, are filling vacancies as mechanics in heaven. The same would apply to my mates in Cliffoney, who loved Elvis and would sing their hearts out on the way to and from dances; again, quite a few of them have gone. I have to say that I can't help feeling a little sentimental.

I read recently that sad songs help us deal with grief more effectively than listening to the rap and boom music that we hear so much of today. The more lamentful tracks you listen to during a life crisis lift the spirit and help us to recover sooner. I really agree with this. Sad songs are a great tonic that help us cope with a negative situation. Music provokes the most amazing sense of recall and, in my experience, listening to an old chorus can instantly reconnect you to moments of heartbreak, love and absent friends. Memories can get a bit distorted with the passage of time, but music helps those of us in our hour of need. Talking of sad songs … they say that if you play a country song backwards you get a happy ending!

As a BBC broadcaster on the *Irish Eye* programme, as well as filling in on various other shows, I find nostalgia and music an intoxicating mix. It can break down barriers and fill the heart with great emotion. What's more, it can instantly take me back home to the music of bygone days. The so-called music 'experts' can talk all they want about a classic melody, a good rhythm, or a song destined to make it big, but the bottom line for me is that the listener sat at home will always be the judge, jury and switcher on or off.

Little has changed in radio presenting over the years in spite of huge advances in clarity and developments such as stereo, digital, internet radio, 'listen again' and podcasts. You switch it on and a voice or tune comes out, simple as that. I have been lucky enough to experience life as a broadcaster and, yes, I love working on radio, but I have loved listening to it even more.

MEETING MY SPORTING HEROES

By the time my radio career was underway I was also fortunate enough to be a columnist for the *Irish Post* national newspaper, writing about things I loved: Gaelic football, hurling and the showbands. I did this on a weekly basis for about fifteen years. It was the most amazing time in my life, enabling me to meet many of my sporting and showband heroes. Poor Sally came along and never once complained.

During my childhood, certain Gaelic footballers and hurlers were gods in my eyes and I idolised them. The great Irish sports commentator, Michael O'Hehir, brought matches alive by describing so vividly the style and grace of such footballing and hurling greats as Padge Keogh, Mick O'Connell and Billy Rackard. Those names were implanted in my mind's eye for ever, but never in my wildest dreams did I imagine I would one day meet them, let alone get to know them personally.

Padge Keogh of Wexford was a true boyhood hero – with my mother's maiden name being Keogh, I grew up with the dream that we were somehow related. Dreams seldom come true but this one did when I had the pleasure of meeting him. We were not related, but what a modest, unassuming gentleman. Padge was part of the great Wexford hurling team of the fifties and sixties that won all the top honours. My visits were frequent when Padge would take me on a tour of the Wexford landmarks and revisit some of his childhood playing areas. When he died, it felt that part of my childhood had died with him.

In those innocent days before blanket television coverage, the three Rackard brothers of Wexford hurling fame grabbed the attention of all sports lovers, and their names still reverberate down the generations. Billy, the youngest, was a marvellous hurler and by the time I got to know him the older brothers had sadly passed away. To give you some idea of their greatness, all three were named in the greatest team of the century. Billy always made Sally and me very welcome and we enjoyed days and nights in his company. Billy introduced me

Me with Padge Keogh at his home in Wexford

Billy Rackard showing me his collection of medals at his home
in Wexford

to many other greats in Gaelic games and, like Padge Keogh, I was
heartbroken when he died.

Kerry's Mick O'Connell was Gaelic football's first superstar. Even
now, nearly sixty years later, his name is spoken with admiration
whenever Gaelic football is discussed. Mick enriched my life with
memories so vivid that they make light of the sixty years since I first
had scissors in hand to cut his picture from the national papers and
neatly place them in my scrapbook among other greats. I had the
pleasure of interviewing the great man on the radio, but never did I
believe I would meet him face to face. I was so excited when the day
came. Along with his lovely wife Rosaleen and their son Diarmuid, we
spent a lovely day and evening in their company on Valentia Island in
Co. Kerry. We even kicked a ball around his garden, which brought
a tear to me eye; not so much for the nostalgia, more for seeing how
good Mick still was, well into his seventies. Thanks for the memories,
Mick.

Another football great was the late Jack Mahon of Galway, who
was also a prolific writer on Gaelic games. Jack would stay with us in
Oxford when he visited Cheltenham every year for the horse racing.

Sally and I meet my football idol Mick O'Connell at his home in County Kerry

When he passed away in Galway, he very kindly left me all his Gaelic football and hurling books.

Sport has always played a huge part in my life, and I suppose boxing and Gaelic games come top of my list. In my mind, however, Mohammad Ali was by far the greatest sporting legend in my life time. I have such vivid memories of listening with delight to the news coverage when he floored Sonny Liston in 1964 to win the world heavyweight boxing title. On the subject of boxing, when I first started broadcasting, I had the pleasure of interviewing the Irish boxing legend Barry McGuigan. He knew I was a bit nervous and did his best to put me as ease, when really it should have been the other way round. A lovely chap and a credit to Ireland.

Obviously Gaelic games take pride of place and you may ask who in my opinion was the greatest ever footballer and hurler. Comparisons between players of the past and the present are not issues easily dealt with. Trying to compare a footballer or hurler with another from a different generation only adds fuel to the fire. Mick O'Connell from Kerry and Mickey Kearins from Sligo were the two best footballers I ever saw. If I was pushed to name my all-time favourites, I would stick my neck out and name Mick O'Connell as the greatest Gaelic footballer of all time and Henry Shefflin of Kilkenny as the greatest hurler. I would love to have met and spoken to famous hurler Christy Ring of Cork. Sadly I was never able to get Christy's contribution – not that he refused, but rather the Grim Reaper intervened and sadly he died a relatively young man in 1979. On a visit to Cork I persuaded Sally that we needed to see a well-known beauty spot called Cloyne. She was used to being led up the garden path when it came to hurling and football, so wasn't surprised to find that this 'beauty spot' was in fact the graveyard where Christy Ring was buried. She had finished her book by the time I got back to the car, having studied every headstone in the cemetery. Bless her!

Chapter Nine

GOING BACK TO MY ROOTS

Now sweetly lies old Ireland
Emerald green beyond the foam,
Awakening sweet memories,
Calling the heart back home.
(Trad. Irish proverb)

GONE BUT NOT FORGOTTEN

They say that once your parents die, life will never be the same again. I think this is true, but I feel blessed to have many special memories of both my father and mother.

By the time he was sixty, Michael was already an old man: the hard work on the farm had taken its toll. On reaching his mid-sixties, and hundreds of miles away from him, his health deteriorated. I found his mental illness very distressing and accepted his life was coming to an end. Here was a man who never raised his voice in anger, a really patient, quiet gentleman. I never once heard him swear and he never had a bad word to say about anyone. In fact, he would leave a person's company if they were gossiping. He also never once showed emotion by hugging you, but I suppose he came from an era when men were men and displaying any tenderness was viewed as a sign of weakness.

Michael was a most unassuming, gentle and kind man and, although he had several fiery children, including me, he never reacted. He was attached to the land, the crops and the animals it nurtured. He knew the farm like the back of his hand and his sudden wayward behaviour, like wandering off and not coming home, caused great concern to the family. Michael had lost his memory and a touch of dementia had set in.

Nancy and the rest of the family looked after Michael tirelessly for years before he died in 1990, just short of his seventieth birthday. His funeral was huge, with the whole village turning out to pay their respects. Gone, but not forgotten.

My mother Nancy, a woman of rare charm, passed away in May 1997 at the age of 69. She was a lady of immense character; everybody loved her. People were drawn by her warmth, good nature and magnetism. As a mother she was there for you, advising and soothing, with the odd kick up the backside to make sure you were listening. Haggling was her thing: she'd arrive home laden with bargains, or what she thought were bargains. Sally remembers one day on the bus when Nancy paid half fare for her and then quickly told her to take her engagement ring off before the bus conductor caught sight of it.

Nancy had a great love for reading and would sit in her chair surrounded by newspapers, magazines and books. Old papers were special to her; she would read well into the night. Anyone who knows me well will know that I inherited this trait from her. When I was young I'd borrow papers from any source and read them, and even to this day someone else's newspaper is not safe should I see it. I still can't resist the temptation to pinch one dumped in a bin, such is my voracious appetite for the written word, and much to Sally's embarrassment.

Nancy also had a great love for the Royal Family and, in particular, Princess Diana. I don't think she ever believed me when I told her that, when I was in plain clothes duty in Oxford standing at a road junction, Diana passed by in a car and smiled at me. In fact, I think she winked at me, but this may be like the cross-eyed girl I once met at a dance.

Nancy, though struck with bronchitis all her life, made light of the problems and very seldom complained about the debilitating nature of the disease. She battled bravely, gasping for breath and on death's door more than once, an inspiration to her family and everyone that knew her. At the end, and in so much pain, she went peacefully and willingly to her Maker. After her death the thing I missed most was my telephone conversation with her every Sunday evening, when we'd discuss the family and the gossip from home.

Nancy lived a lot longer than I ever imagined. Her great charisma will never die to those of us who had the privilege of calling her mother. We all loved her.

BACK TO CLIFFONEY

The tranquil village of Cliffoney has changed somewhat over the years, as you might expect. The church and primary school are still busy, although the layout and structure of both have changed quite a bit since I was skipping through the doors.

Of the three local shops, McGowan's is now closed, with only the shell of the old building remaining; Timoney's has been refurbished and turned into living accommodation; and McCannon's is now a bed and breakfast business.

Despite closing its doors many years ago and moving a short distance up the road, the old Garda building is still there, and can be identified by a Garda indent above the front door. Nowadays, though, the police station, or barracks as it was known, is gone, together with the last guardian of the peace. A bit like Oxford, things have gone from one extreme to another, with the nearest police station located miles away and out of reach to people who need it at short notice.

The doctor's house is still there, but these days is used as a day centre for the elderly.

The dentist, who owned the crochet school, later sold up and opened a craft shop by the school in the village. He was a real character, with a quirky sense of humour, so much so that when he died the family had his headstone inscribed with the words: 'Now filling his last cavity.'

Although for obvious reasons solemn places, graveyards and, indeed, funerals can be places of great humour. I remember one time in Oxford, when most of the mourners had filtered out of a funeral, some of the locals went to their family graves to say a few prayers. One fella I know looked at his father's tombstone and was heard saying, 'That's where I'll end up, if God spares me.'

The village post office has historically been one of the most utilised buildings in any town or village; however, these days the post office is contained within the local food store. Our post office mistress, Kathleen Clancy, only died in recent years, having lived to over a hundred years old. The old post office building still stands, but is now a craft centre.

Public houses remain part of the fabric of Cliffoney; however, the historic and atmospheric boozers in the village today are outnumbered by those which have closed. Out of the five in my time only two remain.

Dunleavy's was the first of the five pubs to close its doors, way back in the mid-sixties. The building has since been developed into flats. Hannon's has long closed and the pub licence sold on; however, the building is still there.

Cummins', one of only two remaining pubs, is now called O'Donnell's and is hugely popular with regulars and visitors alike.

Harrison's, where I worked as a teenager, continues to be a popular place with both the locals and visitors. A succession of my family worked there after I left, most recently my nephew Darren. Michael Harrison died in his forties, a great loss, not only to his family but to the village as a whole. For a number of years after Michael's death it was run successfully by his wife Dympna, and these days it's an award-winning restaurant and bar run by their son, Declan. Little did I think when I was belting out songs as a teenager that in years to come my son Duncan and his girlfriend Karen would be entertaining some of

Duncan and me 'performing' in Harrison's pub, 1995

the same customers there, whilst on holiday. They were advertised as 'On tour from England – one and only performance in the north-west of Ireland'! In fact I was delighted to give a song myself – due to popular request of course!

And finally Clancy's public house is now closed, but the building with his name on is still there. Although landlord Hugh Clancy died many years ago, his memory lingers on.

The interior of pubs has also changed since my time. In the past, many covered the floor next to the bar with sawdust, which was to mop up the spit from customers who chewed tobacco or snuff – hence the phrase 'spit and sawdust pub'. All sounds a bit crude now, but a very common sight to be seen during my youth. In addition, back in the fifties and sixties, it was a very male dominated affair, so much so that some pubs even had small enclosed areas called 'snugs' where female customers could drink in privacy. These days, like so many pubs, they sell more food than beer and are more of a family affair.

And finally what about Mullaghmore? Has it changed since my dreaded donkey racing days?

Well despite the passing of time, little has changed in the way of

My brother Michael with Duncan and Stephen in Harrison's

developments in Mullaghmore; the two hotels, namely the 'Beach', which has changed hands more often than the shifting sands, and the 'Pier Head', owned for many years by the McHugh family, are still there and holiday cottages are dotted all over. Gable stone walls remind me of a time long gone. The face of the rural landscape has, however, changed, with much of the woods vanishing to be replaced with fields of green grass, and beef cattle peacefully grazing. Gone too are many of the old fishing boats, to be replaced by pleasure craft and sailing dinghies.

To this day I continue to enjoy walking along Mullaghmore's sandy beach with my family, taking in the sights and sounds and thinking about old times. Watching the sun go down on the Atlantic Ocean in Mullaghmore is a sight to behold. It continues to bring the romance of the place to life and makes you feel lucky to witness its rugged glory.

CLOONKEEN – 50 YEARS ON …

Cloonkeen always had a vibrant little community when I was

growing up, and the rural tradition of 'looking out' for each other was commonplace. In many ways, this is still the case today. When I return these days, I often take the time to walk along my old road and reminisce about what things were like, and the many people now long gone.

At one end of the road were a family by the name of O'Brien. The house is still there and used as a holiday home. Lily was the only one of the family I went to school with.

Next came a large family of McGoverns. I knew all of them from my time at primary school. The family uprooted and moved to New York in the late sixties. The shell of the house remains, opposite the place of my birth.

Further along came the Wallace family of seven. I was very friendly with the two boys, John and Pat. John sadly died before his fortieth birthday. Pat, one of the most caring, generous people you would ever wish to meet, lives in Sligo town and I see him regularly. We were the best of friends, and Sunday afternoons would see me out in the road waiting for the boys to show over the brow of the hill with their self-made hurling sticks and a small ball, sometimes made of paper. We'd spend hours bashing the ball around trying to play like our hurling heroes. Before he died, John built a bungalow near their old house, where he lived with his wife Helen and three children. Helen still lives there.

John Wallace

Pat Wallace

John McHugh lived in a small little house, on an acre of land. The gable walls are all that remain.

The Farrell family were the salt of the earth. They had nothing, but never complained. I walked to school with all their children. The older members are dead and gone and the younger ones scattered all over the place.

Very close to them were husband and wife Frank and Maggie McSharry. They never had children. Frank kept goats; you could smell them miles away. The old house was restored by Brendan, a chap from Dublin, who lives there now.

Next was a running stream which ran under a tiny little bridge. You would hear the water flow as it dripped to a lower level and I believe it was known as the 'puddle'. This scene unfolded hundreds of times when my father, Michael, told the story of headless men appearing and howling like wolves in the darkness of night. Even now, should I walk by the stream at night, I never look towards it, in case I see something.

Our house, now owned by my younger brother Michael, is further along, and next to it lies the full shell of a house which stood there in my father's childhood days. He never saw anybody living there. This old house was a really great place for us when we were growing up, with many hours spent climbing the walls and running through the grounds. Come each springtime, the front garden and ditches were smothered in wild primroses.

The shells of two more old houses are dotted further along, which grieves me when I think of all the hardship endured by families long ago. With rampant emigration, many left for far flung lands, never to return again. Again, the old gable walls are all that remain.

The gable wall is all that's left now
The old thatched cottage has fallen down
I dry my eyes as I fondly remember
The days of long ago when I was young
(Kevin Sheerin)

The Barrys were a proud family who kept their property and gardens in immaculate condition. I was very friendly with their son John and daughter Mary, who were more or less the same ages as me and my sister Mary. The house now lies forlorn and empty. I walked to school with John and spent most of my time in his company either playing marbles or ball games. We still meet and reminisce about the old times.

Charlie Watters' two storey house stood out more like a stately home. It had a blue slate roof and dormer style windows. A long laneway from the road enhanced its looks. These days this once lovely house is now starting to crumble. Charlie was a bachelor farmer until late in life when he married a local woman, Maggie. It was there that his nephew stayed the night before he was killed in a traffic accident. I heard a banshee cry that same night. In Irish folklore the banshee is a spirit that is heard to cry when a death is imminent.

The McCannon family lived up a long laneway. There were three bachelor brothers, Denny, Patrick and Bernie. All three were fond of the drink, but harmless enough and good neighbours. Bernie, the youngest, had such a way with words that, at times, you'd have thought

Close neighbours, Tommy and Tony Kenny

he had swallowed a dictionary. Unfortunately, however, he would have difficulty pronouncing the big words and people used to laugh at him. He was very funny and we, as a family, would always defend him. The old house lies empty, with a padlock on the half door.

Maggie McGovern was the oldest resident living there in my time. She lived alone and was still in good health when I left for Oxford. The day before my departure, she handed me a little card with the word 'Jesus', and a prayer on the back. She told me to always keep it with me and I promised her I would and, to this day, it's still in my wallet. Maggie's daughter, Margaret, married my uncle Dan, and it's pleasing to see her grandson, John Wymbs, built a holiday home where the old house stood.

Jimmy Mullaney was another bachelor farmer who spent as much time in our house as his own. He would arrive in the evening and stay until midnight, especially in the winter time. A clever man as he didn't need to light his own fire to keep warm.

A new house, the property of Mary Barry and her husband, stands on part of their family farm and is used as a holiday home.

The last house and one I enjoyed visiting was Kenny's. I only remember the three sons, Joe, Tommy and Tony. Tommy is still in the village and can be seen most days speeding along on his bike leaving a cloud of dust behind him. Sadly Joe and Tony have passed away. Tommy reminded me recently of my exploits going to dances some seven miles away on the crossbar of his bicycle. In his own words I neither had any money or a bicycle to ride.

And finally to the crossroads, another running stream and more ghosts if you'd believe Michael. Pigs with two heads frequently drank from the stream and would chase you in the dark. Tall stories indeed.

Only four new homes have been erected in Cloonkeen since I was a child.

BUILDING A NEW HOME

I had always longed to build my own home in Cloonkeen, where my family and I could spend time during my retirement, and now the time had come to do just that. First, however, I had to convince my brother Michael that I deserved a complimentary building plot on the farm as it's what my parents would have wanted. Unfortunately he didn't fall for that old chestnut, and after weeks of looking at different house plans we chose one which we liked. My brother Thomas, no slouch when it comes to making money, was more than keen to take on the building work and sub-let the carpentry to my brother John. Fine by me. Sally and I helped with the foundations and, when finished, Sally looked like 'Rambo' – muscles everywhere. Our intention at the time was to build a smallish little bungalow, but Thomas convinced us that size matters (I'd heard that one before). We visited regularly and in 2000 the bungalow was up and ready to live in.

The site was my former playing field next to the farmhouse, and overlooking the sea and the mountains. We spent three months there one summer, sorting out the gardens and building a long stone wall to the front of the bungalow. My brothers, who are fine tradesman, couldn't believe the quality of my stonework. Mind you, my ten-year-old nephew Ryan was the brains behind it!

As for decorating the house, not long after my brother Pat finished painting every room, I decided that the house would benefit from a photo gallery of football, hurling and showband heroes of yesteryear on the wall of the stairs. After a couple of dozen black and white picture frames, I stood back and decided that the wall still looked rather bare and required more of the same. Originally I assured Sally that only one side of the wall would be used for this purpose but, to her despair, the pictures spread like wildfire. My granddaughter, Maisy, tells me she has counted three hundred and fifty pictures, and that number is still rising. Even though I say it myself, the pictures look great and are admired by everyone. I'm not finished yet, though, and my next book will reveal all.

While not adding to my ever-expanding picture collection, I was witnessing bees causing havoc outside. Being raised on a farm and subsequently having a love of gardening, I have had my fair share of stings over the years. There's nothing quite like that horrible stabbing needle-like sensation. Not surprisingly, I have become quite cautious when it comes to wasps and particularly nests, which, as we all know, can be very dangerous.

Anyway, I am not the only family member that has fallen foul of our buzzing little friends. Moreover, there's an old expression 'don't stir up the hornets' nest', which my brother Pat can certainly relate to. For safety reasons, I had for many years badgered him to place a manhole cover over a three-foot water connection, which had become covered with grass and weeds. First it had to be bricked up, and then sealed over by a metal cover. Having reluctantly agreed to do the work, Pat entered the hole in shorts only to be attacked by a swarm of wasps. He was stung all over his body and needed immediate medical attention. I later tried burning the wasps out but singed my hair in the process, leaving the wasps angrier than ever.

Following Pat's traumatic experience, others in the family have also shown themselves incapable of dealing with these little critters in a safe, practical and humane way. My brother-in-law, John McGovern, for example, had his own method, which is a story we still laugh about to this day. On being made aware that there was a large wasp's nest in my garden, John proceeded to march across shouting for everyone in the immediate vicinity to move out of the way and enter the safety of their homes. Confusion quickly turned into panic as, without warning, John pulled out a double barrelled shotgun and fired a barrage of shots straight into the unsuspecting swarm of wasps. The nest and part of the garden were blown to smithereens and, alas, all but one of the wasps are rumoured to have escaped!

(Un)fortunately the fun and excitement in and around our house is not confined to land. On a recent visit, we ventured out for an afternoon's fishing in Mullaghmore with my cousin Anne and her husband Graham. Now Sally is not much of a sailor, but didn't want to miss out on the fun, especially as the grandchildren were going. The party of eight of us, together with the boatman, got about a mile out when the sea erupted. My daughter-in-law Karen was frantically looking for life jackets and Sally was trying to take photos before turning a funny shade of green. I was holding tightly to granddaughter Maisy, who was more interested in her fishing rod and the number of mackerel she was getting on her line. Similarly, grandson Danny, together with my nephew Aaron, were slinging their hooks out to sea without a care in the world. The sea was so rough even the boatman said we should turn back. I've never seen waves like them and I was scared, but the children loved the occasion and wanted more. To round off a frightful day, I spent a fortune in the pub on our return when the women ordered double brandies all round in an attempt to settle their stomachs. Mind you, despite stinking the house out, the fish tasted nice!

I look forward to taking my other grandsons, Harry, Archie and Ralph, out when they are older, but I don't know if Sally will brave it again! Stephen and Alison love to bring their children to spend holidays in Cloonkeen and it's really nice for me to see them there and playing games in the same fields where I played all those years ago. They love to visit their family and Alison has a keen interest in the history of the place, which is lovely for me.

OLD ACQUAINTANCES

When returning back to my home in Cliffoney, I occasionally get the chance to meet up with people I haven't seen for years, and sometimes even decades.

In the 1980s, some twenty years after leaving the vocational school, I happened to bump into my mechanical drawing teacher, whilst enjoying a pint in the village (you will recall he was the chap who I had clashed with at school). He immediately recognised me and enquired about my life since leaving the 'tech'. At that time I had great pleasure in telling him I was the police sergeant in charge of the Didcot area. I could tell from the expression on his face and comments that he was surprised and delighted. Little did I know then, but he had worked on the huge power station buildings in Didcot for two years at its inception. From his ramblings he obviously knew the area very well. What a small world!

Another character who has reappeared from my childhood is Tipperary native, Sergeant John Hennessy, who was posted to Cliffoney village on promotion in 1960. A tall, no-nonsense man, he provided my personal details, including height and family background, to the police authorities in Oxford when I applied to join Oxford City Police. Now retired and still residing in the village, I am delighted to say that I continue to enjoy meeting up with him, reminiscing about the old times and life in the different police forces. John remembers telling me that if I chose to apply for the police in Oxford, even if I didn't get accepted I could always say that I had been to Oxford! Another friend from the police I am still in contact with is Brid Wymbs, a distant cousin and near neighbour from Kinlough. Interestingly, Brid was one of the first woman to join An Garda Síochána in 1959.

More recently I have enjoyed a happy reunion with Maurice, the chap who was hugely instrumental in my initial application to join the police whilst working in Maye's Motors. Fifty years after working together in the garage, I was visiting my sister Ann, getting my hair cut, when she mentioned that Maurice was one of her customers and would like to see me. On my next visit over, we met up and discussed how life had panned out for both of us. I must admit I'd forgotten that Maurice left for London the same year as me, when he joined the Deutsche Bank. In fact, he came to Oxford and walked the beat with me during a day shift and managed to find himself a bed in the police station for a couple of nights as an invited guest (not as a convict!). Maurice rose to a senior level in the bank and retired in the late eighties. He then joined the Essex police on a short-term contract as a community beat officer. Who would believe that, as we joked about joining the police way back in 1967, both of us would end up doing just that?

While in England, Maurice kept in touch with home and was an avid reader of the *Irish Post*, paying particular attention to my scribblings. These days he is retired and enjoys his gardening and his love of reading. Married with four children, Maurice is still the same laid-back chap I knew from my garage days and it was lovely to rekindle old memories of times gone by.

It really is a dream come true to have built my own house on part of the farm where I grew up and also to be able to reunite with friends and acquaintances from my youth. As a teenager I clearly remember bringing home some type of spruce sapling on the handlebars of my bike which I then planted outside the front of my parents' house. This tree is still to the front of the house and, despite constant trimming, is now over twenty metres high and hangs over the side wall of our garden. What's more, fifty years later I'm burning the cones from it on my own turf fire. Now, as I watch them burn brightly, a smile comes to my face remembering the good times.

MY SIBLINGS

Being one of a large family is in itself rewarding and having a house there also means that I can enjoy the company of my siblings and their families on a regular basis. In fact I see more of them than I could ever have imagined, which is great.

They are all blessed with a natural gift of patter, which makes them fun to be around. There's an

Mary and Mick

old saying, 'family and friends are the medicine of life', which certainly rings true for me.

My sister Mary, who is a couple of years younger than me, was the only one of the family to follow me to live in England, where she trained and qualified as a nurse in Birmingham. We got on really well as children as we shared a lot of the same interests but, unfortunately for her, she has been the butt of my pranks over the years.

Mary had a dreaded fear of mice and paid the ultimate price by telling me this. One day I discovered a dead mouse and couldn't resist the temptation to place it in one of her shoes while she was asleep. Right on cue, I heard this almighty scream in the morning as she placed her bare foot into the shoe completely unaware of what lay in it. Her having never got over the experience, I must admit that I did regret this incident.

Another time when I was a teenager, white socks were all the rage. Anyway, after getting back from working on the bog, I had dirty black feet but couldn't be bothered washing them prior to going to a dance. Instead I simply borrowed Mary's one and only pair of white socks, which left her with no socks for school the following morning.

Mary was brilliant around the house, as mother was always sick and in poor health. She cleaned, cooked and looked after the younger children.

Pete and Esther

It was in Birmingham that she first met her husband Michael McBride, who was a postgraduate student at the time. After their wedding in 1978, they set up their first home in Newcastle. It was there that Mary took up a post as a nursing sister at a National Health Service hospital. Her nursing career spanned 47 years. They are now returning to live in Sligo.

Pete was next in line and is much thought of in his adopted town of Roscrea in County Tipperary. Always with a smile on his face, he is one of the most caring and generous of our family; a good-humoured man who radiates enthusiasm and optimism.

He was tall, had the looks and could charm the birds off the trees. What's more, he was the only one of us with an arse, and would get teased about it. His reply was always the same, 'It takes a big hammer to drive the long nail.' Enough said.

Pete was a very good athlete and footballer in his youth and won numerous medals for running. His forte, however, was arm wrestling, when he'd take on and beat men twice his age. His upper body strength, from heavy mechanical work, ensured his hobby of arm wrestling took on a new lease of life in later life. I took him on once when he nearly broke my arm. I'm pleased to tell you my lad gave him a run for his money by nearly beating him on one occasion; mind you, there was a twenty-five-year gap in age.

After national school, Pete attended the nearby vocational school, before working in a garage in Sligo town as an apprentice mechanic. He then moved to Tipperary to further his experience and worked for many years as a lorry and machine mechanic, covering a wide area, doing repairs on broken down vehicles along the roads.

The 1960s proved a great year for Tipperary hurling and a chap by the name of Kieran Carey was one of their star players. I hated Tipperary at the time but, incredibly, Pete's daughter Paula is Kieran's son's partner. I had the pleasure of meeting Kieran on a number of occasions before he died. A lovely man.

Pete married a Tipperary girl, Esther, and they have four daughters, Michelle, Paula, Laura and Caroline. He loves the bog, and in summer months he can be found talking to his turf and fixing old tractors.

Pat was always careful with his money and from childhood made the rest of us green with envy as he watched his piggy bank grow; from all accounts he still has his Holy Communion money. It was well known among the family that, when he was young, he kept his savings in a box which he locked. A little bird now tells me that, unbeknown

Pat and Sheila

to him, some of the siblings devised a cunning plan to get into his box and steal some of his money.

Pat still retains close links to the family farm and in his spare time has a passion for old farm machinery, especially tractors and ploughs.

I would describe Pat as a grafter who's always on the go. Accordingly, if he says he will do something, rest assured, it will get done. What's more, nobody knows the landscape and woods around Cliffoney like him. He appreciates what nature has given to us and has a special relationship with the sea and mountains. To travel a journey with him is much more than to traverse the highway.

He cycles miles from mountain to sea on most days of the week and is as fit as a fiddle. Despite his impressive fitness levels, as a youngster sport and Pat didn't mix; in fact, he was so bad he couldn't kick 'snow off a rope'. I recall that on his first visit to us in Oxford back in the early eighties he got me into all sorts of trouble by lashing a leather football so hard in our small little patch that it landed four gardens away, breaking branches off delicate trees and the neighbour's finest roses.

Pat attended Grange vocational school and worked in the local pub during holidays. He then got a job as a store man at a garage in Sligo town, and has been involved in similar work ever since. He is currently store manager of a Scania garage outside of Sligo.

Pat married a local girl, Sheila, and they have two daughters, Lisa and Valerie.

Rumour has it that Thomas is the wealthiest of the family. He was born in 1956; from all accounts, a birth that almost killed Nancy. According to her he was a sickly little chap, and was the bane of her life with his antics when he lived at home.

He lived in London for a few years from the late eighties and became a frequent visitor to Oxford. Around this time, I became friendly with a plumber who worked at Eton College in Windsor. Thomas was in the right place at the right time and got a decent job there. It was also

Thomas

during this period that, as he will acknowledge himself, he had an uncanny resemblance to Diego Maradona, the famous Argentinian footballer. I recall on one occasion I was with him and some friends on a visit to Madame Tussauds wax museum in London. With Thomas having disappeared, we continued our tour into the sports section, only to find him standing still as a mouse amongst the sporting elite impersonating Maradona. We were all in fits of laughter when a young chap attempted to touch his hair only for Thomas to nod his head at him. Completely baffled, the poor chap ran off in a panic shouting 'he's real!'. I should point out that Thomas has never been a football fan and anyone who has witnessed him on a football field will know that his footballing skills are, in fact, more akin to Madonna, the pop princess, than Maradona the footballing great!

Another thing I learnt is that you never allowed Thomas to walk in front of you in a shopping area or street where there were large glass windows. He would suddenly halt, step back, glance in the reflection of the window, and preen himself, allowing the poor fools walking behind him the embarrassment of crashing into him and everybody else.

Thomas stayed with us on several occasions, including an enjoyable Christmas in 1991 when I made use of his handiwork and got him to do all the plumbing on our new bathroom. He enjoyed the work in England and made enough money to return to the village and build himself a beautiful home, which he later turned into a thriving bed and breakfast business, called Atlantic Haven.

After three boys, Joan was no doubt a welcome addition to the family. She was a good twelve years my junior and I remember her being very tall and smart. She has a lovely way about her and was always very generous when Duncan and Stephen were small. In the late seventies, when she was only about seventeen she came over to see us, taking the train from Birmingham to Oxford. She was very brave to do this at that young age as I don't think she had ever ventured out of Ireland before. I met her at the station and she stayed for a few days.

Joan worked in the local shop for quite a while before marrying a Leitrim man, John McGovern. They have a family of three boys, Damian, Darren and Ryan. She keeps herself in shape by walking and cycling every day. Now a permanent fixture at Abbots (a global healthcare company) in Sligo for over 30 years, the company have awarded her work and achievement with trips abroad and no doubt big bonuses, which she denies.

Joan and John

Joan and John built a new house near the old family home, and we enjoy their company when we visit. Like Nancy, Joan adores her garden, which is a credit to her, with its design and colourful landscape. A motor mechanic by trade, John's now semi-retired and enjoys nothing better that re-building old tractors and walking his dogs. He is a marvellous storyteller.

My brother John is very well read and a great conversationalist. Although I never saw him play, I'm led to believe he was an excellent footballer in his youth. When I was fourteen, I became his godfather; I probably owe him a fortune for missed birthday and Christmas gifts which somehow got

John and Geraldine

lost in the post. A carpenter by trade, John is now self-employed and one of the most sought after tradesmen in the village.

He is appreciative of the landscape around him and, like Joan, is a keen walker and cyclist. His only weakness lays in his support for Manchester United. It was John that passed this to my son Duncan and subsequently to my grandson Danny. During our Christmas holiday to Cliffoney in the late seventies, John was a firm favourite with the kids, taking them out on the tractor and spending time with them on the farm.

I have fond memories of John and his wife Geraldine coming to stay with us in Oxford in 1990; it was great to see them. Having lived in the village all their married life, they have two children, Amanda and Mark.

I scared the life out of John recently by telling him about ghosts and things that go bump in the night, and where they hang out. I understand he's now reluctant to walk on his own near the spots in case they appear. He assures me that, if he sees one, he will face them bravely and tell them to leave him alone. I've come to the conclusion that John is scared of things that go pop in the night.

Tina, God love her, was the first of the family to pass away as a result of that awful scourge, cancer. She was only in her forties when she was diagnosed and died in 2013. She was married to Rory and was

Tina and Rory

a proud mum to Tracey, Linda, Orla, Sandra and Warren. When I left in 1968 she was only three years old, so we didn't know each other that well.

Tina was a very private person, who kept her thoughts to herself. She set up home about four miles from where she was born and worked in various jobs. Highly intelligent, with a lovely sense of humour, she was a look-alike of mother, with the same temperament.

A gorgeous looking girl who loved her flowers as well as her family, we were pleased to see her at Stephen and Alison's wedding and enjoyed spending time reminiscing about her childhood. Sadly, a month before she died, her daughter Linda passed away in tragic circumstances.

Tina faced her diagnosis of cancer with astonishing bravery and calmness, often thinking of me rather than herself. I was so pleased to spend some quality time with her before she passed away. May the bed of heaven keep both of them warm.

A lovely brother, but not the earliest riser in the morning, Michael is one of nature's gentlemen, laid back to almost sleep mode. Following our father's death, he took sole ownership of the farm and was a great comfort and company for Nancy.

At this stage, he appeared to be a confirmed bachelor, although never short of friends, male and female, being such an amiable chap. He was six months old when I left for Oxford and, like Tina, we didn't know each other that well at the time. I remember him as a gorgeous little boy with blonde hair, who wouldn't eat his vegetables. As the years passed, Michael's gentle manner and personality made him a favourite with everyone.

Holiday time gave us the opportunely to get to know him better, but he would disappear into the fields rather than say goodbye when we left to return to England.

Michael and Tracy

Michael was always great with children and it was wonderful when he met and married Tracy and had a family of his own (Aaron, Sophie and Elsa). I was delighted to be the best man at their wedding.

Ann is the youngest of the family and as the baby was spoilt rotten. She was not born when I left Ireland and is nearer in age to my own children and sometimes behaves more like my grandchildren! (Only joking Ann!)

During holidays to Cloonkeen when Duncan and Stephen were primary school age, Ann would have the record player out and the three of them would be dancing around the farmhouse. I remember Bruce Springsteen's 'Dancing In The Dark' was the big hit at the time and was played endlessly.

After attending school, she trained as a hairdresser, which has turned out to be a great blessing. When we are on holiday we get a haircut with a dinner thrown in (all at a discount!). Ann is the most generous person in the world and is a great cook – always able to dish up a lovely meal at short notice.

Ann and Timmy

I never thought, after the demise of the country

showbands, that I would live to see my baby sister following the same path and with even greater enthusiasm, attending dances all over the area with her fiancé Timmy.

Ann is a great hairdresser and has her own salon, building up a substantial business over recent years.

She is mother to Edele, Sharon and Steve.

At Michael's wedding: Thomas, Joan, Pete, Tina, me, Michael, Pat, Ann and John

Chapter Ten

My Family

In this chapter I want to say a few words about the nearest and dearest people in my life, all of whom have filled me with an overwhelming sense of gratitude.

I've had a wonderful life, blessed with the love of my life, Sally. Our sons, Duncan and Stephen, and their wives, Karen and Alison, have given us so much pleasure; they are great to have around and we are now lucky enough to have five grandchildren nearby to keep us on our toes. Hopefully they will care for us in our old age and won't have to spend all of their inheritance on a care home!

I remember thinking, when I first set eyes on Sally, that anyone can catch your eye, but it takes someone special to catch your heart. Sally

Me with Sally outside our house in Cloonkeen in September 2016

Sally snaps us at the circus: me with Ali, Karen, Stephen and Duncan

has always been there for me and we enjoy the simple things in life, like family and the garden. I'm so proud of her transition to radio, which she took to like a duck to water.

Sally is unassuming, modest to a fault and honest, with a great sense of humour. She is a great wife, mother and grandmother, and we still have a lot of fun together. In fact, we are a good team. The other good thing about her during our marriage is that she is a great one for sorting out the nuts and bolts in putting flat pack furniture together! Unlike me, she will read the instructions first and then direct the operations, telling me where things should go. She has also been a great one for taking photos, even from when we first met. This drove me silly at times, but I now appreciate the record of our life together.

Duncan, our older son, was first to tie the knot, by marrying his sweetheart, Karen. Duncan originally worked in finance after leaving college, but in recent years trained as an occupational therapist, which he thoroughly enjoys. Karen is a music teacher and singer. They have obviously followed in my footsteps as they also perform as a duo (hopefully they will do better than I did)!

In 2002, our first grandson, Danny, was born, which was a great delight for us. His birthday is 11th November, the same date as my

Our grandson, 'Danny Boy',
October 2016

Our granddaughter, Maisy, in
Mullaghmore, June 2016

Our grandsons Harry, Archie and Ralph on the farm, August 2016

own birthday and that of my father. Danny is very musical and plays the trumpet, piano and drums. My favourite granddaughter Maisy – bless her little cotton socks – arrived a couple of years later in December 2004 and, apart from being a daddy's girl, is my girl as well. She plays the cello, and has a fine singing voice. Maisy has taken part in many school productions as well as dancing on stage.

Stephen, our younger boy, married his darling Alison in 2004. Alison comes from a big family and her grandmother came from County Tyrone.

Stephen currently enjoys working in publishing and has become quite a handyman in the garden, building his own potting shed (must take after his old man!). Alison started up her own HR recruitment company some years back and is doing well. (I always ask her how much money she is making but she is cute enough to keep it to herself!)

They have given us three lovely grandsons. Harry was born in 2007, wait for it … on the 11th November too. He wasn't due for another week but, according to Alison, arrived early due to her laughing so much at my sister Mary's 'drama queen' antics at my 60th birthday party the night before. Harry is a very bright, caring little boy, who enjoys his rugby, street dance, and playing the violin. Archie was born in July 2009, is extremely funny, destined to be a comedian, and has already shown promise as a footballer by playing for the local team. Ralph came along in January 2016 to complete their lovely family. I'm told he has my nose. We can't wait to see what he gets up to.

Ralph's christening in May 2016

Epilogue

Two things are certain in life: we die and we pay tax. If I could, I'd avoid both. Death has always fascinated me from a young age, and graveyards are a place I often visit. Sally is testimony to this rather odd behaviour. On many occasions I've taken the poor girl to some far-flung lands to visit the graves of famous footballers and hurlers. My family in Ireland worry about this strange 'hobby' and say that I'm not right in the head. I suspect that their concern is less about my wellbeing, more the fear that I will come back and haunt them. One day, I may just do that.

Talking of death, if I were to write my own epitaph it would read, in the words of Waylon Jennings (1978):

> *I've always been crazy and the trouble that it's put me through.*
> *I've been busted for things that I didn't do.*
> *I can't say I'm proud of all of the things that I've done,*
> *But I can say, I've never intentionally hurt anyone.*
> *I've always been different with one foot over the line,*
> *Winding up someone, even those who are one step behind.*
> *It not been easy, but I guess I shouldn't complain.*
> *I've always been crazy, but its kept me from going insane.*

In March 2016, on Stephen's thirty-ninth birthday, we visited Eynsham Hall for lunch. It is now a smart hotel and conference centre. I had not been back since I left Police Training College back in 1968 and, despite a flower roundabout preventing anyone from parading on the front driveway, the 'big house' hadn't changed; it was more or less the same as when I left. The oak panels and stout doors were still intact, as were the large classrooms, and I could still smell the coldness and loneliness where I endured months of torture all those years ago. Funnily enough, police memorabilia was neatly displayed in glass cabinets, some of which I remembered from my earlier days as a new recruit. Seeing this made me smile, as it reminded me of the way old relics and fossils are displayed at the famous Oxford museums. I've certainly been called an old dinosaur in my time, but never thought my original police uniform would be part of a museum collection!

Returning back to Eynsham Hall was a special day and I really enjoyed my trip down memory lane. In a way, I suppose it was the catalyst for getting on and writing this book as, together with the birth of my little grandson Ralph, it made me reflect on my past, present and future.

Having now reflected back at my twenty years growing up in Ireland, I can honestly say that all my memories are good and I never wanted for anything. Growing up in the village was a full life – Gaelic football, the church, farming and outdoor activities. I thought there was no place like it and I suppose now, looking back, there wasn't.

Nowadays, when I am back in Cliffoney, I take the opportunity to walk along Cliffoney beach and find a peace and solitude in this lovely land of rugged peaks, gently rolling hills, lush valleys and long sandy beaches – a thousand miles away from city life.

As for my life after crossing the Irish Sea, I enjoyed a long, happy and fulfilling career in my thirty years in the police force, which gave me a good standard of living. Every day was like being on holiday; if I could, I would do it all over again. The police force did, however, change my outlook on life: I became more suspicious of people and would see what others did not see or chose to ignore. Once the uniform went on, it never came off. The difficulties of dealing with tragedy, bizarre human behaviour and violence have been ingrained in me. These were the burdens of the job.

During my time in England, I have been fortunate enough to live in one of the nicest parts of the country and over the course of almost fifty years have met some lovely people. These include work colleagues, social friends, both Irish and English, and wonderful neighbours. I couldn't have asked for a better life.

Regrets are few. Perhaps I could have tried harder to move up the career ladder in the police, but I didn't and have no major regrets on that one. Presenting the *Irish Eye* radio programme over the last twenty years, with the recent support of Sally, has been, and continues to be, a fun and entertaining part of my life. I feel blessed and privileged, especially as the radio has always been such an integral part of my life, going all the way back to my days listening excitedly with my family to the wireless in Cloonkeen.

I have no doubt there are some who see me as somewhat extraverted and full of myself. Nothing could be further from the truth. There are few people who really know me, but plenty who think they do. I've always believed in fighting my corner and yes, I've often spoken out when the diplomatic thing would have been to keep my mouth shut, or hit out when others might have counted to ten.

As for my health, thankfully it has always been good, apart from the 'old knees', for which I blame Sally for not taking more care of me when she was a student nurse. I finally had a knee replacement in 2008 and, despite some discomfort, I'm still here, moaning and groaning about getting old and suffering from back pain and tight shoulders. These days, when I wake up in the morning, I always pinch myself and, if it hurts, I know I'm still alive. In the evening I then read the obituaries in the *Oxford Mail* and if I don't see my name I know I'm in the land of the living.

I sometimes ponder on those 'what if' moments; those funny twists of fate that have ended up shaping my life. For example, what if my friend Maurice hadn't applied for a police application form on my behalf? What if I hadn't picked out Oxford City Police when choosing from ten police forces written down on screwed up bits of paper? What if I hadn't found the slip of paper with an unknown telephone number and made the call to find out it was Sally? Fascinating, really, when you think about how quickly life can change direction. I have to say that I never dreamed for one second, whilst laying under a dirty old car in Maye's Motors nearly fifty years ago, that my life would turn out to be such a roller coaster of fun and enjoyment.

As for the future, I've forgotten about the pipe and slippers and intend to embrace my seventies – I believe that later life is for living and to be celebrated. Every day brings so much pleasure being around those I love. As the saying goes, 'the older the violin the sweeter the music'.

Now, as this chapter ends, I look forward to the next chapter in my life.

May the road rise to meet you,
May your journey be sweet,
And may God hold you in the palm of His hand.
Until we meet again.

(Trad. Irish Blessing)

Malinmore Head

Rossan Pt B.
Glen Columb

Malin B.
Malinmore
St.
League
16.
Kil

Rathlin O'Birne I.
Malin Hd.
Carrigan Hd.
Teelin B.
Kil

Malin Beg
Fintrag
Mc Swy
St. Joh

Do
Mullagh
Mille H

Inishmurray

Streedagh Pt.

patrick Hd.
Creevagh Hd.
Benwee or Kilcummin Hd.
Lenadoon Pt.
Carrickadda Pt.
Coonamore Pt.
Sligo
Brown B.
Benbulbe

Lackan B.
Killala
Bay
Easkey
Bay
Aughris
Drumclif
Ballysadare B.

en
fram
B.
Bartragh
I.
Easkey
Dromore
Kn

Inisherone
Knockalongy
1278
ns Gou

alla
Roggerie
Abbey
Corbally
L. Easky
Mountain
1635
Collaney

Ballina
SLI
1383
1331
L. Talt
Ballynacarrow
Templehouse
Ho.
L.

Sl. Gamph
1036
Aclare R.
Moy
Tobercurry

Knockmore
R.
Banada
R.
Carrowillan

Hd
Foxford
Moy
Curr